Universal Warrior Arts System

Spiritually Motivating Inspiration for Self Defense

By

Grandmaster Austin Wright, Sr.

SIDEKICK Publications 2013

Mission Statement

The mission of the Universal Warrior Arts Federation of America is to service, promote and teach educational, practical, and disciplined "Combined Martial Arts" to students, through U.W.A. concepts and principles. The main goal or purpose of the U.W.A. is to incorporate a self-defense system that can be utilized in a prevention/intervention crisis situation. This is accomplished through verbal and peaceful resolution, which instills self-control in a student, as opposed to taking out one's aggression on another human being. Negative energies are sublimated by the U.W.A.'s self-defense techniques thus better preparing students for various hostile or threatening scenarios. U.W.A. techniques divert excess negative energy through self-discipline. One can use this practical art for sport, street survival, health benefits, or even in a working environment (i.e., law enforcement, nursing, and education). The Universal Warrior Arts System can be utilized by all.

Purpose

Be not wise in your own eyes nor recreate the wheel. Instead, be open minded and seek to incorporate and "individualize" the secrets of Universal Warrior Arts which has been passed down through "Three Generations of World Champions training World Champions." A living legacy inspired by a higher power. The U.W.A. Martial Arts lineage is derived from Asian Martial Arts roots that have branched into America.

Table of Contents

Table of Contents

Table of Contents

Table of Contents

WARNING!!!

This book is only to be used as a guideline for combined Asian and American World Martial Art's History, Prevention, Intervention, Safety, Battlefield Readiness, Knowledge & Rank belt advancement. Any facsimile of items printed is due to the nature of terms that are used and universally accepted in Traditional Martial Arts training. In regard to physical training, all students are required to train under a certified Teacher/Instructor for direct supervision and application of the U.W.A. System. The U.W.A. System's Founder, Teachers and Representatives will not be held responsible for any misuse of this book and its applications.

For inquiries about registering your school or dojo under the U.W.A.
Federation of America,
Contact the main headquarters.
Universalwarriorarts@yahoo.com

At various time in our life, "we will be under attack by the enemy" whether you're walking to your car, your home, by a Bully, Addictions, Terrorist, at work, in your home, verbally and spiritually.

However, you can prevent your opponent from defeating you through Defense, but you cannot defeat him or her without taking the Offensive.

-Sun Tzu

"Don't wait to be a Victim, Be a Victor!"

THE FIGHTING SPIRIT

The *"Old Age"* Soldiers/Warriors (Teens and Adults), of yesterday are the "*New Age*" Warriors of today. They must balance the raising of a family with work and duties of Self-Protection, Self Defense and Safety of the Mind, Body, Spirit and Intellect. They are everyday heroes.

The New Age Warrior is a person who will nurture their family to the best of their ability, hold down a job, consistently meet their responsibilities and represent the Martial Art cause. The Fighting Spirit must be both determined and able to adapt to change. I believe in Action and Re-Action. I am a mover, who believes in cause, effect, and results. I believe that you can take the invisible and make it visible if you Will!! ! I believe that emotion stirs up commotion and commotion is a source of emotional energy that can be seen in the physical as "dramatic action." Being humbled, I have learned that true spiritual power comes "not by Might, nor by Power, but by my Spirit," says the Lord...*Zechariah 4:6.* Spirit builds the warrior within. In Japanese, the inner spirit is called Ki and in Chinese Chi.

I believe and think that the Holy Spirit of God guides us to the Universal Light and is constantly challenging "Resistant Spirits."

By Grandmaster Austin Wright, Sr.
A Seeker and Spiritual Warrior

Dedication

To my Father and Mother, Dennis A. Wright, Sr. and Mary Wright. To my children, Austin J. Wright Jr., Priscilla Y. Wright and Gabriel Wright. To Mr. Antonio Wilson and Mr. Chet Kaminski, Chief U.W.A Instructors, and to all the instructors and student members of the Universal Warrior Martial Arts System.

ABOUT THE AUTHOR

Grandmaster Austin Wright Sr., aka Soke (Founder) is bonded to work in the State of New Jersey, and certified to promote Black Belt instructors, Sensei (Teachers), and Hanshi (Masters). He is an author, Founder and President of the U.W.A. Martial Arts Federation of America. Grandmaster Austin Wright is a national and international Grand Champion and numerous time National Champions Coach and Trainer Austin Wright is the creator and promoter of the Universal Warrior Arts System. He is a Notary Public for the State of New Jersey, a Private School Educator, and Coordinator and Director of several clubs providing Self-Defense/Cardio Kickboxing programs in Hudson County, New Jersey, Pennsylvania, North

Carolina and Italy. His community involvement includes working with the Drug Elimination Program (D.E.P.), being a board member of the Bayonne Youth Center, and the Bayonne Housing Authority Youth/Teen Summer Camp and Karate Program. Wright is the New Jersey State Director for the US National Marital Team "Alliance." He also served as the VFW Post 226 Chaplin, Vice Commander, and Quarter Master. He has been inducted in five different World Marital Art Halls of Fame. In 2005, Wright was a three time world gold medalist and World International Grand Champion. He is a motivator and man of respect and principle. Grandmaster Austin Wright is an advocate for "at risk" kids and teens, wherever there is a calling.

He was born into Martial Arts as the son of a first generation martial arts teacher. Though second generation born, he was first generation trained. His first formal traditional Karate and Judo-Jujutsu training started at age five, under the direct supervision of his father and teacher, Head Master Dennis Austin Wright Sr.

In those days, children did not progress quickly in belt ranking, nor were children given the status of Junior Black Belt. Young, Austin's training consisted of structure, respect, techniques, sparring, form and much of repetition. Trained at a traditional Isshin-Ryu Karate School, his father/teacher taught him his Judo-Jujutsu and American Kickboxing skills privately at home, in the park, and in the hallways of his apartment building. His father also provided private Sunday afternoon classes in their former dojo and in Hudson County Park.

Founder, Austin Wright Sr., has instructed self-defense to military veterans, police officers, school teachers, doctors, nurses, health clubs, children's organizations, security, personnel, businesses, public schools, universities, and private associations. Shihan Austin Wright, his instructors, and students have presented over three hundred demonstrations for educational and instructional purposes worldwide since 1983.

Grandmaster Austin Wright Sr.

International World Grand Champion

PREFACE

The Universal Warrior Arts System (also known as the U.W.A. System) was founded by Grandmaster Austin Wright, Sr. He introduced this system to the Martial Arts World on September 27, 1998. The concepts, principles and philosophy of the U.W.A. System were strongly influenced by Grandmaster Wright's *Sensei* (Teacher) and father *HANSHI* (Master) Dennis Austin Wright Sr. The U.W.A. System was created so that Karate *Ka's* (Students) would learn a variety of Martial Arts disciplines in one *"American Made Self-Defense System."* The idea of having an *"American-Made Self-Defense System"* was not a new martial arts concept. Grandmaster Wright incorporates "all" that he studies into a constantly evolving "Art" (U.W.A.) that will continue to progress and be competitive.

Grandmaster Wright had a "combined Martial Arts" vision for America Martial Arts World. He dreamed of pursuing his vision, believing it was his duty to continue the Wright's family legacy. In spite of numerous attempts by the opposition to stop him and his Sensei (Father), Grandmaster Wright's dream became a reality. Courage and confidence is an ingredient that all champions possess. Grandmaster Wright knows how to win and coach students to Grand National Championships and World International Championships.

In the U.W.A. System, students devote more time to training in order to become a well-rounded martial artist. Karate Ka's achieve balance by being trained in an instructional setting that is formal and disciplined, all the while maintaining the crucial elements of tradition and practicality. This system is implemented under the direct supervision of U.W.A. Certified and Professional Black Belt Instructors. The core of the system was developed initially for "self-defense" and "sport" competition. This style resulted from three decades of disciplined Martial Arts training, two decades of "sport" competition, and the evolution of partner training. Conflict (war) and resolution (peace) play an integral part in the inner cohesiveness of our emotional, physical, and spiritual expression in the U.W.A. style.

The U.W.A. Martial Arts Federation of America was founded in January 2001. Its board members, who are the "Sanctioning Body," consist of community leaders, a doctor, former armed force veterans, educators, a legal advisor, a law enforcement officer, and veteran Black Belts. The U.W.A. System focuses on the improvement of character, as well as martial arts knowledge, both of which will prove to be assets in the life of the student.

This book was written after witnessing random acts of violence, student hostility and anger, active attacks of aggression and incidents of street survival. These experiences and knowledge gained, have enabled Grandmaster Wright to help students re-direct their anger and hostility in crisis situations. This information is practical and designed to empower students, parents, victims, and local law enforcement officials.

This book will provide strategies to strengthen and maximize your God given potential, empowering your emotional, mental, physical, ethical, legal, moral, and spiritual warfare in acts of survival *of the fittest and acts of valor,* through methods proven in street survival and the arena.

What Kids, Teens and Parents Need to Know about Self-Defense and Self-Protection

How to develop self-defense strategies against mental, physical, emotional, psychological and spiritual warfare. Everyone needs to learn Safety Skills and Practice practical Self-Defense.

Everyone needs self-defense strategies against mental, physical, verbal, emotional, psychological and spiritual warfare attacks.

The knowledge contained in this book will spiritually inspire, motivate, and empower you to face your psychological and physical challenges. It was designed to help you understand and maximize your potential, by incorporating that which works best for you. One does not need to always engage in physical confrontations. For instance, if X (any adversary) engages you or shows you signs of conflict or war (verbal, sensed or physical), thwart the lure and show X the door...

There are so many unexpected life crises, personal challenges and battles that families have to deal with on a daily basis that can become overwhelming. Prevention and Intervention Strategies are the key. Families should learn how to "resolve their personal challenges or issues successful".

Be assertive, be consistent, be firm, be fair, be reasonable, be humble, be able to adapt to change, be compassionate, be loving, and sometimes, be able to compromise. You have to give a little, to get a little....Reciprocity.

The Bible says, "Train up a child in the way he should go, and when he is old, he will not depart from it." Proverbs 22:6; "Judge not, that ye be not judged." Matthew 7:1; "You hypocrite, first cast out the beam out of your own eye, and then shall you see clearly to cast out the speck out of your brother's eye." Matthew 7:5.

Kids, teens and families need to defend themselves from the start. Do you fear for your life? How do you deal with threats, gangs, hostile situations, bullying, spiritual warfare, cyber bullying/texting? Do you have any Verbal Ju-jitsu skills? Do you have a plan of action if confronted or attacked by any form of weapon, knife or gun? First you should try to run or try to escape! Use common sense. Only defend yourself if necessary as in an act of desperation. SAFETY FIRST!!!

From the beginning, with God's creation of the Heavens and the Earth and Man (Adam and Eve) was placed on the Earth, we have had constant personal challenges, requiring self-discipline to deal with our personal fears and emotions. Face your fears and life's oppositions. Confront them before it is too late.

Adam and Eve had to deal with the sins of trickery, manipulation and seduction by the Devil, tempted to take and eat an apple from the forbidden tree. Jealously was introduced in the story of Cain and Able. Cain was jealous of his Brother Able and later killed his brother. He tried to hide his sin from God, but God knows all things…Eventually, his sin was brought out to the Light and Cain had to deal with the consequences of his actions.

Be Like a Child at Times

Parents should not forget what it feels like to be young at heart. Think about Matthew 18:1-5, "Be Like a Child at Times". In the Book of Matthew, the disciples came to Jesus and asked, "Who, then, is the greatest in the kingdom of heaven?"

He called a little child to him, and placed the child among them. And he said: "Truly I tell you, unless you change and become like little children, you will never enter the kingdom of heaven. Therefore, whoever takes the lowly position of this child is the greatest in the kingdom of heaven. And whoever welcomes one such child in my name welcomes me." We should remember our youth and what we did when we were young at heart. As a *young energy spirit* myself, I can say that some parents have forgotten what it feels like to be young. Parents can sometimes be so hard on the youth, and critical of their own grandchildren that sometimes they don't allow "kids to be kids."

If you are fortunate, you will get a second chance to live vicariously through another child or their eyes. Remember the magic? If you don't, you never had it and it's time to discover it for yourself. It's awesome! You become their best fan, motivator, cheer leader, and mentor and later, they will be proud to bring their friends to you, knowing they will not be judged.

Not everyone you associate with is bad, unless you are running with a bad crowd. If you are running with a bad crowd, are you really similar to or like them, or is it who you think you want to be? Remember, "Who you want to be, you usually become" If you act like a gangster, you can become a gangster. If you act like a doctor or a lawyer, you can become a doctor or a lawyer you truly can become whatever you choose.

In truth, some have already made a decision in their life. Some kids might already be visualizing the outcome of their future. Some kids are living in the moment. Some kids are carefree and reckless. Other kids say, "I don't know" or "The future really doesn't matter." It may be very difficult to change their perspective. However, it is not impossible. If there is a will, there is way.

"Ultimately, Enhancing the Character is the Key To Training Mind, Body, and Spirit!!!"

INTRODUCTION

A Need for Battlefield Readiness 101

Do you really know where your children are 24 hours in a day? Do you want to feel safe and secure? Have you lectured and prepared your children for Street Survival in terms of Cyber Bulling, School Yard Bullies, Strangers, Gangs, Sex, and Drug Awareness?

It is necessary for the safety of the Mind, Body, Spirit, and Emotional Battles. So if you paused or said no, then this book is vital for implementing an individualized strategic "Plan of Action" that works for you and your family. Why? As we look around today in society it is more obvious or evident that people are more vile and belligerent in regards to their behavior. Think about it! If you agree there should be a feeling of expectancy that should have engaged and intrigued your Mind and Spirit.

That is, if you are universally connected like branches or leaves on a tree as many of us are in the Martial Arts World. There are many safety topics that kids, teens, and parents ought to know. I incorporated an arsenal and strategy guide to protect against physical, mental, emotional and spiritual assaults made by the enemy.

Family Safety, Personal Survival, Wellness and Spirituality are some of the basic needs of Life. It starts from birth and until we pass on or depart from earth in the physical sense. We, who have faith in the Super Natural Spiritual World believe we are not just fighting or struggling with sin, or each other, but against invisible principalities...

This is my "Supernatural" thinking and reason for writing this book. It is to prepare and defend your family from the start! Believe! And you will see...Strengthen your God given potential through Safety 1st and C.H.I. (Character, Humility & Integrity) training. Our goal is to Prepare Our Leaders for Unlimited Success to include having a winning Positive Attitude that anyone can possess.

As an Educator, we teach Social Interactions, Confidence, Safety Skills, Emotional Health and Life Skills. I believe all Parents and Martial Art Instructors should teach or learn Self-Defense, understand and implement Prevention and Intervention Tactics of Karate, Kick Boxing, Ju-Jitsu and Judo Combative Art Principles. Our mission is to improve our

Verbal Ju- Jitsu and Self-Defense Strategies daily. Coming up street smart while traveling worldwide for the last 35 years, no matter where I went, I continued to hear about, read about and see, good descent people and their families being victimized, attacked, bullied, tricked and assaulted World-Wide. People were being verbally and physically attacked despite the victim's willingness to comply with the thugs, gang members, thieves or drug dealers and their request to give them the money. The media and newspapers give the grim, bizarre and tragic truth of these endings of their life stories. Despite public awareness and warnings, kids, teens, and parents are still under attack in the world by various enemies. Not just in the physical sense but in their daily walk, conversation, emotionally, socially, spiritually, physiologically, and psychologically speaking. We in the Spiritual World believe we are not just fighting or struggling with sin, or each other, but against invisible principalities...

So, the objective of this book is to teach you sophisticated strategies, to stop, deter, or intercept an attacker. In order to stop the enemy or deter them, you need to see things from a universal perspective or the big picture.

Some of us have changed our social economic environment by leaving the ghetto, which means you were fortunate enough to break away from the chains of poverty, adversity, ignorance and oppression. This means you have made a choice and sacrifice for the next family generation to come. Later, once success is achieved, you are now able to give back to the community. There is an old phrase that says, "You can take the kid out the street, but you can't take the street out of the kid". Understanding that phrase, it has prepared me for Life Skills, Street Survival, and Wellness. Self-Defense Tactics and "Real Deal" Street Wise Strategies that have been proven in Warfare, Street Survival, Life Skills and various arenas. It is Vital, for Life Skills Survival.

Family Safety – How this is achieved?

I say, Get Fit! Get Strong! And Get Results! Practically is Emphasized, Defend and protect yourself and kids. Prevention is key! Practice Safety Drills and Hypothetical Scenarios in an Exercise. Like a fire drill, you need to practice Self-Defense drills, like playing your favorite Video Games to build strategies to beat the game. Makes sense right? It is similar to playing video games that contain Real Life Simulations and experiences engaged in combat. The games teach you and require you to maintain and create your own Personal Counter Attacks and to have knowledge of strategic codes for use of "Element of Surprise" to beat the game.

Remember there is "Power in Words", Meditation, Inspiration, Faith, Self-Motivation and Self-Encouragement. It is about Quality vs. Quantity in terms of Technique, Practicality, and Results.

We must achieve our Goals in life. Practice the rule of consistency. If at first you don't succeed, try, try again. While trying to succeed, you need to maintain this behavior consistently while staying fit and spiritually and emotionally strong the entire length of your life. Have a Positive Attitude And "Never Quit!"

Finally, we must attempt to preserve a healthy ecosystem and environment for our future generations to come. Take care of Mother Earth and your family. Later, they will take care of you (Universal Law). More importantly do not become anyone else's pawn. "Be a mover, in the Game of Life". Also don't wait to be a Victim, Be Victorious!

CHAPTER 1 - *The History*

An Overview of U.W.A.'s Beginnings

1985

While serving in the U.S. Air Force, I organized and established a U.S.A.F. (Seymour Johnson Air Force Base) Karate Club for military personnel and their dependents. The experience of interacting with universal martial artists from different Armed Forces in the North Carolina area helped me achieve another level of leadership and enhanced my martial art skills. These experiences broadened my horizons and opened my eyes to a whole new level in martial art and self-defense techniques.

1988

After a three-year tour in the U.S. Air Force, I was honorably discharged with a Good Conduct Medal and a burning desire to create my own system. I studied military politics, military science, and combative arts and principles. I joined the USAF Reserves at McGuire Air Force Base, and volunteered for Desert Storm. Although I did not see any combat duty, I was a dedicated Soldier. The war ended quickly and I was released from the Inactive Reserves as Sgt. E-4 in the early 1990's.

1990

After returning to civilian life, I opened my own dojo in Bayonne, New Jersey. Later, I went into partnership with my father, and opened the Dojo of Self-Defense for competition and educational purposes. During this time, I received formal clinical training while working at Bayonne Hospital's Physical Therapy Department and Psychiatric Ward 5(b) for several years. Prior to that, I worked at the USAF Seymour Johnson AFB Hospital in Goldsboro, North Carolina, rotating through the entire hospital for training as an AF Medic.

1996

In January 1996, the partnership (Dojo of Self-Defense) was dissolved and both my Father and I went our separate ways. I continued to expand my efforts in Kissimmee, Florida and Hudson County, New Jersey.

1997

Upon my return to Bayonne, New Jersey, my ongoing desire to introduce my new style continued to increasingly manifest. My loyal Board Members and I knew it was time for a radical restoration of style and a new beginning. So we made a pledge, and went forward in the face of all opposition.

1998

My new style, known as *Universal Warrior Arts* was introduced to the Dojo and students in September 1998 (aka "The Birth Year"). The new U.W.A. System consisted of new forms, basic exercises, kicks, and eclectic Judo, Jujutsu, Kung Fu, and American Kickboxing.

Universal discipline and respect became a big component our organization. 1998 was also the year that we publicly announced our intentions to our former associates, which did not make them very happy. My father felt it would be better to take responsibility for my own actions, failing or succeeding on my own. Now as a recognized Master and Soke (founder), my Instructors and members and I would only be under my sanctioning. It was a clean break and a new beginning.

1999

The year 1999 was the year of the Incorporation of the Universal Dojo of Self-Defense, AKA Wright's Universal Dojo. (See Appendix - Press Release on Wright's Family Legacy, 1999).

My Father and I decided it was time to take a public photograph to substantiate and validate our Wright Legacy Claim/Legal Parting of Dojos. We wanted to let the public know that he gave me his blessing and permission to fly on my own to promote, certify, direct, and sanction all business decisions, concepts, and U.W.A. Principles.

2001

Years in the making, the sanctioning body known as, the **U.W.A. Martial Arts Federation of America®** was officially formed. It was established to sanction, recognize and certify students, instructors, teachers, coaches and members of honor.

2004

Team Wright was scouted and pre-qualified by Dr. Jim Thomas, Head Coach for the U.S. National Martial Arts Team "Alliance" to compete at The World International "Freedom Games" competition held in Jamaica International.

2005

Grandmaster Austin "The Technician" Wright Sr., won three gold medals and the Grand Championship Belt at the Freedom Games International Competition.

While several of my team members also won World Championship titles, including my son Austin Joel Wright and daughter Priscilla Yanery of the Wright Legacy.

2008

As Grandmaster, I was awarded an Honorary Ph.D./Ma.D.Sc, Doctorate of Martial Arts Philosophy and Martial Arts Science from the University of Asian Martial Arts World Study in March at the U.S.A. Hall of Fame dinner.

From left to right:

Nick D'Anna, Black Belt Instructor at the Bayonne Soccer Club, HANSHI Dennis A. Wright Sr and Grandmaster Austin Wright Jr.

History, Background, and Comments

on the Legacy of

Grandmaster Austin Wright, Sr.

By Josie Cleary

Grandmaster Austin Wright Sr. was born on January 7, 1965 in Jersey City, New Jersey. He was the second son of Mary U. Kelly (Irish American) and Dennis A. Wright (African-American). Austin was raised in Bayonne, New Jersey. He lived in the Bayonne Housing Apartments with his five brothers, Mother, and Father. Grandmaster Austin Wright Sr. was introduced to the martial arts at the age of five by his father Hanshi Dennis A. Wright Sr., himself an accomplished master. In succeeding years, a lifetime of wisdom and knowledge was passed down from father to son in such varied arts as Judo, Jujutsu, American Kickboxing and Isshin-Ryu Karate.

After graduating from Bayonne High School in 1983, he enrolled in Essex County College, Newark, NJ for a year and a half. Wright realized, however, it was time to move out, to move up. The U. S. Air Force became his home and training for several years. He continued his college coursework while in the Air Force. He married at age 19. At age 21, his son Austin Jr., was born on the U.S.A.F. Base in Seymour Johnson, N. C.

From the age of fourteen into his early 40's, Grandmaster Wright won numerous first through third place championships in Kata, Kumite, and Weapons. He performed in a demonstration with his father in a cable television documentary titled, "Bayonne's Martial Artist," narrated by his father Master Dennis A. Wright, Sr., in Bayonne, N. J. (1982). Wright was a fast learner and by the age of 18 was a black belt instructor at the Bayonne YMCA Summer Day Camp and the Bayonne Military Base Dojo.

When he followed his desire to serve his country in 1985, he transferred his now considerable teaching skills to Seymour Johnson Air Force Base in Goldsboro, North Carolina, laying the foundation for his first karate club in the process. Throughout his competition years (1979 – 2005), he won numerous awards, including the Sergeant's Open Karate Championship in North Carolina, the Red Dragon's Karate Society's East Coast Karate Championship in Pennsylvania, Gary Alexander's Metropolitan Karate Championship, the Metropolitan Institutional Karate Championship in New Jersey, Johnston County Karate Championship in North Carolina, as well as the Invitational Open Karate Tournament and Karate International, both in New Jersey. As a lightweight and middle weight champion throughout the east coast, Grandmaster Wright was known as the "*technician*." His fast hands, expertise, spinning kicks, and thrusting techniques were noted for fracturing ribs in and outside of the Dojo. Grandmaster Wright's reverse punch incapacitated many of his opponents and sparring partners and his jumping vertical leap could surprise his larger 6-foot opponents. His natural ability to sweep his opponents to the ground, score points, and win *Kumite* (sparring) competition came from training with his father and four brothers (Dennis Jr., David, Daniel, and Dwayne Wright) at an early age. Grandmaster Wright was a full contact fighter, known in the United States as a "superb fighting technician." His father and teacher was a strict, disciplined, and serious warrior and trainer of many champions as well.

In September 1996, Grandmaster Austin Wright Sr. was honored by various members of his former Karate Association, as well as the Drug Elimination Program and numerous other groups for his twenty-five years of service and dedication to the "Martial Arts World." One of his achievements came on September 26, 1997 with formal recognition by a high ranking authority, Grand Master Don Nagel, for his outstanding loyalty and devotion to the martial arts world.

In 1997, he made a commercial for Dillin Tire Company, and in 2000 and 2001, choreographed and acted in commercials for Wright's Universal Dojo of Self-Defense, Inc. In October 2002, the Bayonne and Jersey City Public Access Channel aired the documentary, "Wright's Martial Arts Lineage and U.W.A. System," narrated by Grandmaster Wright.

In 1999, board members of the Universal Dojo of Self-Defense, Inc. honored Grandmaster Wright as the outstanding Instructor of the Month in a public press release.

"His commitment and willingness to stick to his vision is astounding," stated Chief Instructor Mr. A. Wilson, a Vietnam Veteran, Martial Artist and an Instructor for the Universal Karate Schools... A paragraph from the book of the Sacred Circle says, one of the problems people have today is that they are not willing to find the river in their own life and surrender to its current. They are not willing to spend time because they feel they grow up trying to please other people and they rarely ask themselves, Who am I? They live in terms of pleasing rather than in terms of being who they are..." Grandmaster Austin Wright, Sr. is definitely not one of those people," said Mr. Wilson. Grandmaster Austin Wright, Sr. has 30 years of active experience in the Martial Arts, is a veteran of the U.S. Armed Forces, several times Champion, and honoree of a very prestigious Entrepreneur Spirit Award given to him by the NAACP."

The Wright Repertoire or "style" is "Universal" because it is not designed for just one particular group, but encompasses all. This new program puts a heavy premium on loyalty, comradeship, integrity, and training. Wright states, "To know oneself is the ultimate goal; to help others is a wise decision. Our philosophy states, everyone has the ability to evolve and develop new ideas. Our program is practical enough in application to allow novices to choose the best direction for their individual development. It relies on the karate-ka's repetitive workout with pre-set solo application or partnership to achieve perfection in kata (form). This new art (U.W.A. System) helps individuals recognize the roots of conflict, understand the importance of resolution, develop a philosophy of life, and finally, achieve a sense of inner peace."

Grandmaster Wright emphasizes that this art was not started to degrade any other styles. "In fact, we take the best of some martial art styles so as to encompass all styles and to benefit the individual as a whole."

"The development of his new system, which he chose to name Universal Warrior Arts, has been for him a source of solace, inspiration, adventure, and delight. He said that he used the word Universal, because the universe encompasses all in existence," said Chief Instructor Mr. Antonio Wilson.

His Universal Warrior Arts System is formulated with practical and street conscious awareness in mind as well as Universal Philosophy and respect for the law. *"Nature does not move in a straight line, neither do I,"* stated Grandmaster Austin Wright.

"His admiration and his devotion to his three children, Austin Jr., Priscilla, and Gabriel, as well as the other students at the Universal Dojo of Self-Defense, Inc., Society Hill I Karate Club, Ferris High School Karate Club, and the D.E.P. Karate Program, goes beyond words," said Chief Instructor Mr. Wilson.

Finally, Grandmaster Wright's formal training in Kung-Fu (Tai Chi Chuan, from the Wu-Shu System) came from a Chinese Teacher from China, named Ms. Jett. She instructed at the main Headquarters of the U.W.A. Federation of America (2001). She was a member of the Chinese Wu-Shu Demo Team.

Grandmaster Wright started the Universal TKO Cardio-Kickboxing classes with his brother, Dwayne J. Wright, who is an amateur N.J. Golden Gloves and Diamond Gloves Boxing Champion.

Grandmaster Wright presently serves as Head U.W.A. teacher of the Jersey City Public Schools Karate League, the Bayonne Public Housing Drug Elimination Karate Program, the Jersey City Society Hill I Karate Club, and Bayonne Police Athletic League Self-Defense Program. He is a member of the Bayonne, NJ branch of the NAACP, VFW Post No.226, National Notary Public Association, and President of the U.W.A. Federation of America.

Grandmaster Austin Wright and his Instructors have a large U.W.A. Membership following and several U.W.A. Clubs throughout the Hudson County, New Jersey area. They are presently recruiting and training students, competitors (Warriors), and teachers (Sensei's) to run and operate their own Dojos (schools) worldwide.

Biography of Head Master
Dennis A. Wright, Sr.

Master Dennis Austin Wright Sr. was born in Bayonne N.J. on September 27, 1942. In the mid 1950's, Master Dennis A. Wright., Sr. (a 45-year veteran of Martial Arts) started his formal Judo-Jujutsu training. It was at the Bayonne Naval Academy, AKA M.O.T.B.Y. He trained under the direct supervision of the late Dr. James Lavender who was a World War II Veteran.

"Master Dennis A. Wright's Martial Arts training helped him excel in football and track during his Bayonne High School years," said his Bayonne High School football team members and coaches. His competitive spirit made him one of Bayonne's greats in track and field during his high school years.

After five years of Judo-Jujutsu training, Master Dennis A. Wright, Sr. ventured into Full Contact Karate (under the Isshin-Ryu System) and Full Contact Kickboxing (N .Y. Puppets). He won two First Places in 1973 in the House of Empty Hands Championship to place 1st in Kumite and 1st in Open Hand Kata, as well as 1st through 3rd during his Tournament competition years. He was picked to make a documentary/video titled ***"Bayonne's Martial Artist"*** in 1982, with his son, Austin, and main disciple which aired on (video on hand for viewing) Bayonne's Cablevision. The documentary included his history, Judo/Jujutsu skills, teaching abilities,

Karate Katas, board and cinder block breaking techniques, his practical self-defense, street survival skills, and his eclectic skills as well, which were passed down to his son, Master Austin Wright, Sr. Master Dennis Wright Sr. taught many of Bayonne's best in Kick-boxing and Karate in the 70's, 80's and 90's. "All who knew Master Dennis A. Wright Sr., trained with him or competed against him, knew of his knowledge, intensity, skills, and dedication (50 years) to the Martial Arts World. Now my father, Master Dennis A. Wright Sr.'s teachings and contributions shall be honored and remembered," said Grandmaster Austin Wright.

CHAPTER 2 - The Philosophy

POSITIVE AFFIRMATIONS

"All one should strive for is to be better than before"

Some students learn this the hard way. I have found that those with an open mind and military training background grasp this concept quicker than most. My reason for developing this style was not to say which styles are best, but to compel my students to see Martial Arts or Karate as a different approach to bettering one's self. Aside from learning the art, it is important that the student work on their personal levels of self-control, self-discipline, self-esteem, attitude, as well as respect for man, woman, children, teens, and the elderly (humanity in it's all). We can never be perfect. Yet we must continue the "struggle" (The Good Fight).

Make a commitment:

"One must choose to bear his/her own cross"

It is the nature of man/woman to resist change, however, if students are to evolve and reach their full potential, while gaining self-discipline and control, they must fight against their old nature and resistance to evolve. You can take someone out of the streets, but his street survival skills will stay with him as well as his social/economic experiences. When he/she is frustrated or angry, the evolved student must use their new self-control methods. Think: What is the right thing to do? One must keep in mind that making the right choice is usually not always the easy route to take, but the necessary one. If you regress to your old ways, then you truly have lost the inner battle of changing one's self.

When overwhelmed, most students regress back to what they know. It takes years of training to change, along with a sincere desire to do so. To avoid regression, one must train both inside and outside the *Dojo* (martial arts training facility). The younger we begin to learn, the easier it becomes to assimilate new skills. Often, children and college students learn quickly due to an openness to learn, infer, discover, evaluate, research, prove, disprove, and debate. School, particularly the benefits of the college experience, afford you the ability to think for yourself. It allows you the freedom to express yourself. It is for this reason that I decided to make the Universal Dojo a teaching/educational dojo, with high motivation and intensity.

"Love what you do, train hard, and train some more...."

Do not let people brain wash you or give you auto-suggestions. Seek truth and the rest will ultimately follow.

John F. Kennedy, a favorite President of mine, who promised to work for freedom around the world, stated to the American people, *"Ask not what your country can do for you,* but *what you can do for your country."* This is my calling as a Martial Artist. I am a promoter and advocate of "readiness" for self-defense. We as a nation must keep America powerful, promoting safe and educational Karate classes/seminars, to assist the "World Humanity Race."

Martin Luther King, Jr., stated, *"I have a dream that my four little children will one day live in a nation where they will not be judged by the color of their skin, but by the content of their character."* For me, this is Universal Diversity. This is why I choose to call my Dojo the Universal

Dojo of Self-Defense, Inc. U.W.A Academy. I choose the word "Universal" because it is *"For All,"* not just a select group.

For years I wasted time asking myself trivial questions like "Why did someone do this, that, or the other to me?"

The simple answer was,

"Why not?"

People have the benefit of free will. We need to stop feeling the need to be in total control of others or certain circumstances. As a mature individual, it is important to recognize that you do not always have control of what happens to you, but you always have control of how you react to it. The idea is to stop procrastinating and find your purpose, wherever it may lie.

"All training starts from the bottom and what you put into training is what you get out of training."

There comes a time in your life when you realize, out of your own spirit or from your mentors, that you must take charge of your life and be productive. Do not give up or surrender. Instead follow through with your goals. Stay patient. Stay determined. If leaders tell you that you cannot do something because you are "socially" or "economically deprived," find a way and seek advice and assistance.

"Eagles fly alone while seagulls and pigeons flock."

Surround yourself with positive people in your quest for progress and when you achieve your goals, come back and reciprocate. My new vision is to see Universal Brother/Sisterhood between all Martial Artists, despite the differences in opinions and preference of style.

Meditation

Why should we meditate? To find ourselves, to regain focus (concentration), to recover (to bounce back), to reflect on negative and positive events, and to produce a positive outcome. Meditation has been practiced for many centuries in countries such as Japan, India, Africa, Europe, Poland, and America, just to name a few.

Who meditates? Serious practitioners and disciples of various disciplines, for instance Monks, Zen practitioners, Buddhists, Spiritual people, and Martial Artists.

There are various types of meditation. A meditation that worked best for me was breath counting while lying down flat and relaxing my whole body from my head to my toes. Once relaxation occurred, I would use the technique known as visualization along with specific goals. I found that breath counting (basic meditation) or breathe control helped a lot while under stress or hostile situations. Visualizing my goals during meditation allowed me to relax and see the end results. Most importantly, I was able to focus on reachable and attainable goals, such as: winning championships, opening my own Dojos, and being a good father and friend to my family and children. I always feel like I am under construction. That is why I continually try to improve myself.

Beware of those who utilize games and manipulation, especially those individuals who constantly display negativity in your presence. For instance, people that make statements such as, "You'll never be this or you'll never be that, you will never amount to anything, or you can't do this or that." Can you change what they say about you? Sometimes, but most times not. Can you change how you react to it? Absolutely! Sometimes "reaction" is the right reaction. Spend less time on whining and more time on shining. One of my mottos is: *"Discipline & Defense. You can't have one without the other."*

Common sense is very important as well. Sometimes you have to know when enough is enough, or when it is time not to engage in altercations or physical confrontations. Peace is resolution and war is conflict. At different levels, we must change inwardly (spiritually) in order to transform our minds and actions outwardly (behaviors).

Resistance to the truth is futile. Everyone is entitled to an opinion or a way of viewing the world, but you cannot change history or turn back the hands of time. One must give praise to a Higher Power and be appreciative for being put back on the right path over and over again, despite the continuing obstacles placed in your way.

Being a reformer and being endowed with a strong sense of orientation, I meditate daily on what path I should pursue. This strategy brought me to the creation of the (hard and soft style) U.W.A. System.

"Truth before Diplomacy"

"All shall start from the bottom of the ladder before climbing up to the top to achieve Black Belt status, thus developing loyalty and appreciation for the Art of the U.W.A. System."

"Constructive criticism is good for the soul as well as for the character…"

Compliment people. Say things like: "You're the Best!" Give people credit, recognize and appreciate all, especially family members. Build people up, do not tear down or criticize them all the time. Say words of praise from a sincere heart.

I believe in Spirit. I believe we can change our ways despite our socio/economic experiences. I believe in cause and effect, and I believe in action. I believe that "accidents do happen." I believe in recovery. I believe in "Peace of Mind." I believe in "Respect for Respect." I believe in "Degrees of Control." I believe in Things to come." I believe in Effort and Results." Don't tell me what you could have or should have done. Tell me what really happened and what your honest goals and/or intentions are going to be. Then pursue it!

Take Responsibility for Your Actions

(Q) Who is responsible for you and your progression in life as an adult?
(A) Hey!,Guess what?   Society and your parents are not responsible for everything, good or bad, that happens to you.

The effort and hard work **you** put into life usually pays off in the end. Your successes or failures are usually the cause and effect related to the right or wrong choices you make on a daily basis. We cannot choose our parents, race, or childhood social class status. However, we can voluntarily change our own path (free will). We all face hardships and conflicts throughout our journey in life. God, duty, honor, family (Dojo) and country should be on your agenda. So stop complaining, fabricating, and making excuses as to why you can't take responsibility for your own progression in life. Now go forth and do what you were born to do!

(Q) How should students deal with life's obstacles?
(A) Realistically, one can look at life's obstacles as an adventure and/or an experience that mentally, physically, and spiritually prepares you for future obstacles.

(Q) What do most children do when they fall down?
 (A) Ultimately they get back up!   Shine, Don't Whine, In the New Millennium Time.

(Q) Why do people believe and express their own lies?
(A) People believe their own lies and express them because they cannot handle the truth.

They rationalize or misrepresent the truth so that they can protect their self-esteem or have someone else agree with them and tell them that they are right. Lying sounds better than the truth and some people arc just pathological liars, or maybe their heart is so corrupt that it blinds them from the truth. It's better to say nothing, or less, instead of telling one lie, then another, to cover the simple truths...All truths are but half-truths...(The Kybalion). There are two sides to every story, and then there is the "big picture,"... This is when extremes meet. (The Kybalion).

(Q) What is relative to us all?

(A) To continue to keep progressing not regressing. Do not be stagnant or dwell on the "Why" too long.

A positive student's attitude usually reflects great leadership. Constant excuses are for those who procrastinate or are quitters. We need to take responsibility for our actions. Remember, there are many windows of opportunity today and tomorrow. Do not be consumed by your failures, nor gloat on your achievements. Learn from your mentors as well as your tormentors. Break the negative cycles (i.e., family problems). Be the navigator of your own ship. Competition is a good thing, however, with this comes rivalries. Beware of those who manipulate, play games, or utilize subterfuge. When you are wrong, admit it, reconcile, and then move on. Look at a person's character but do not be quick to judge. Dream but do not live in an illusion. Train the mind, body, and spirit. Be a team player and have sportsmanship. Keep God above man. Do not be ashamed of being a spiritual individual. Represent your family with honor. People don't just listen to what we say day to day, they usually watch our actions or what we do every day. A good student reflects a good teacher(s). Remember the Golden Rule – *"Do unto others as you would have them do unto you."* Make a commitment NOW! Be productive and enhance a new you.

The pursuit of happiness can come from many things. Health should be first on your list, because without it fear of death or sickness can be like a heavy weight holding you down from flying. Anticipation of death or near death experience can also turn someone in the opposite direction. Near death experiences or incarceration can be a motivating light for people who initially demonstrate negative characteristics. Speak the truth and do not agree or patronize liars or martyrs. Pleasures can make one happy for the moment, but what happens when the novelty wears off? Unresolved iniquities can cause an imbalance within the soul. Obligation to duty and taking care of your personal/family responsibilities is important. If someone shows you war, you show them the door. Addictions, vices, and wrongful temptations must be minimized and eventually overcome. This is your personal goal. To overcome your "old-natured" self and be better than before.

Be conscience of your daily diet, physical exercise, and who and what you are listening to, viewing, and reading. This will help you develop knowledge of the right plan that works for you.

Secrets to Self-Progression

(Q) Can you change your way?

(A) Grandmaster Wright believes most can change who "choose" to or really want to. However, you must understand words like commitment, sacrifice, defeat, failure, rejection, triumph and victory.

1. Don't worry about everyone else's business. Focus on you. Know yourself and voluntarily change yourself. Try navigating your own ship. Stay on your course. If you come off your coordinates, adjust! Quickly! Reset your course to get back to your goal. Like boxing, if you get hit with a good punch, you must quickly recover and come back stronger to dominate and get back to your game plan or eventually you will get "knocked out!" Then you have a harder time staying in the game. <u>Be consistent in all that you do, but do not be predictable.</u>

2. Visualize the caterpillar (as your old natured self, ready to change. Make the commitment to come out of the cocoon, to evolve and mature the mind, body, and spirit. Then imagine transforming into a butterfly, the person whom you would like to be, someone who is intelligent, secure within one's self, courageous, loving, and free to be. This will help to enhance character.

3. Don't make New Year's Resolutions; make daily, weekly, and monthly goals for yourself.

4. Know your purpose early in life (Don't hang out too long). There are many ships that can carry you to the coast, but beware of the Titanic.

5. Later, the rest of life's puzzle will surprisingly fall into place. See the big picture.

6. Try not to blame everybody else for your mistakes. Take responsibility for your actions and choices. Admit to human error, and move on! Be mature about it! Stop playing the Victim or Martyr game. In Psychology, they call this "projection theory."

7. When you greet people be on "alert" and try to make eye contact. Be pleasant and have a serious and optimistic attitude. Have good posture, smile, and release positive and warm Karma (energies) outwardly. However, if people show you signs of "war," be prepared for action (verbal/physical) and thwart the "lure."

Remember, you cannot always change what you are going through. However, you can change how you respond or react to the circumstances or information you receive. For instance, I can choose to be happy or I can choose to be sad. I can choose to be angry or I can choose to dismiss it and move on. Notice, it is true that people who are angry hang out with angry people. People who are happy hang out with happy people. The old saying, *"Birds of feather flock together,"* usually is true.

Remember, it is always better to learn something verses learning nothing.

The Mountain Climb

During one of Grandmaster Wright's annual climbs up Mount Washington in Gorham, New Hampshire, he saw the infinite beauty above and the beauty below. He saw faults in himself and others around him. Then he saw strength in himself and in the teamwork of others. On this he pondered:

Summits surrounded by clouds. The distance seems far, yet each step I took brought me closer to my goals. I was above the clouds and at the top. I felt the infinite beauty of the mountain, **earth**, sky, **wind**, and the sun **(fire)** and inner-self **(iron)**. Streams of **water** (from the summit) were flowing down the mountain. Many thoughts and sensations raced through my mind.

"Nurture first (Discipline) and Nature second (Defense)"

The purpose of the Wright Repertoire or "forte" is self-evaluation and discipline for self-improvement.

Respect for Respect

Most people should try to avoid unworthy altercations. Arguments or disagreements can cause interpersonal conflicts. When inter personal conflicts are not resolved, or dismissed, they can cause some people to begrudge you. Do not take on someone else's personal prejudices or follow evil doers. Do not become a product of a negative environment. Be yourself and adapt. Respect for Respect. Disrespect comes from lack of self-control, anger, and/or a bad attitude.

To gain admiration or respect, students of the U.W.A. philosophy should evolve daily. Individuality is good, but the real goal of the Martial Artist is the coming together of all students, without regard to race, gender, social class, or style. This is a universal Karate Ka. Universal Karate Kas allow "all" to keep their own personality and be creative so as to adapt within a particular society, environment, arena, and dojo.

Kata is a way of expressing one's self. It shows confidence, attitude, stance, technique, determination, weakness, strength, and knowledge of the "Art." The U.W.A. System uses a variety of forces in the Wright Kata Repertoire such as pushing, pulling, spinning, bouncing, rolling, and faking.

In the U.W.A.'s "Art" we take techniques from the kata and use them for self-defense, sports, and training for the mind, body, and Ki (inner spirit). Change your thinking first! Open your mind to fresh new ideas! Learn old and new practical concepts. One cannot have inner peace unless one is willing to evolve one's self. At times, you want to be like a "sponge" soaking up the new and old wisdom then squeezing it out when necessary. As a military veteran, I like to use word pictures, while explaining lessons to my students. This way one can see the big picture and point of view from their individual stance.

Street Survival

To be prepared for every situation is not always possible, however, having a plan is half the battle. The best way to win an altercation is when one does not have to fight to prove your point. If you are under siege, you must attack or retreat when there is no other means of avoidance. Everyone ought to know how to defend themselves, their family, their land, and their principles. If an adversary engages you with a challenge, be ready to go to combat, but try to negotiate peace or resolution first. Use what we call *"Verbal Jujutsu,"* meaning the push/pull/ pull/ push balance theory. "Agree to nonviolence" so as to put out your "fire" (the anger or bad intentions) before it spreads. At this point, you are parrying or redirecting negative Karma. However, if the adversary does not become calm, then you must act according to the circumstances or type of siege. For instance, if there are people shooting guns at you, common sense will tell you to get out of there.

Anger Awareness

(Q) Do you hit first, ask questions later? Do you scream loudly, tantrum, curse abusively, start swinging, or lose your temper?
(A) If so, then you should exercise more self-control and composure. When you are calm, try to pacify a situation verbally. Look for a solution (peace) vs. conflict (war). Also, use intelligence, logic, empathy, and be mature.

If you think positively and do not panic under crisis, or hostile situations, then you are calm. If you are a complainer, whiner, and/or become easily stressed, overwhelmed or frustrated, then you are the opposite.

Anger can be sublimated through Traditional Martial Arts Training. We perform free style or continuous sparring to manage our anger. First, we teach students to develop self-control. Next, we identify emotional triggers, the strongest being anger or rage. Anger is an enemy that does not allow you to relax or focus during adrenaline *"Fight or Flight"* release. Instead of focusing on your strategic game plan, you become frustrated and distracted. Your concentration is off. At this moment, you are not at your best, which means you are vulnerable and open to mistakes and an attack. Fear can make you freeze. It can paralyze you and sometimes cause you to relive, mentally and emotionally, past traumatic experiences over and over.

True thinking, is thinking that is not influenced by fear, anxiety, worry, or emotional distress or personal issues. It is free from all distraction, including people and the noises of society.

Projection of Anger

Be aware of people who do not take responsibility for their negative actions. This includes, kids, spouses, family members, friends, and co-workers. Here is an example:

When reprimanded for negative actions, instead of focusing on themselves, they talk about what everyone else with a similar issue is doing, so as to take the focus off of themselves, and thereby, not taking responsibility for their actions or showing any remorse. In addition, when they are angry with someone else, instead of resolving the conflict with that person, they carry the anger with them and take their anger out on the next available person for no apparent reason.

Emotional Awareness

As humans, we are made up of three things: the will, emotions, and the intellect. Increasing personal emotional awareness and taking initiative help you to reach your goals. Our emotions tell us how we are feeling on the inside. Thus you can be progressive, not stagnate or regressive.

Oppositional Defiant Behavior

Seek God first, because in the Bible, it is written, "*We live in a nation of rebellious people which walk in a way that do not trust God, but instead in their own thought (No Holy Spirit to guide them or open their eyes)."* In other words in their own self-righteousness and beliefs. Not in Truth!

Disrespectful and oppositional defiant individuals think and say things like, "I Dare You! "Or "Make Me!" verbally or subconsciously. They love to challenge and talk back to authority figures such as parents, teachers, coaches, etc. They do what they want to do, when they want to do it, they are disrespectful to anyone in authority. Some signs of this inappropriate behavior include:

• Spoiled – Childish, selfishly demanding behavior.

• Wanting the last word - Argumentative, whining, and complaining.

• Wanting to be right all the time – Blaming others, not taking responsibility.

• Screaming or acting out – Temper Tantrums.

• Constantly making excuse after excuse for their mistakes.

PSYCHOLOGICAL AND EMOTIONAL WARFARE

Who is in charge of your life? Who is in charge of your children? Do you dictate to your kids? Or do you play friends and let them dictate and make demands to you? If you have allowed your kids to be a friend, has the relationship become abusive yet? These are questions that you have to answer for yourself in order to take charge of your life and become the navigator of your children's future success. Do not learn through fear and doubt! Instead, be fearless and have faith!

Working in clinical and educational setting for most of my workforce years, I have discovered only you, can fix you, through self-discipline. However, you must understand your behavior in order to improve yourself. For example:

Impulsive Behavior: Ask yourself one question: Is it an emergency? When you want something that you do not really need, ask yourself: Is it an emergency? Do I need or want this? When someone asks you for a favor and you have not checked your schedule, sometimes we say impulsively yes or no without thinking. Instead say: can I get back to you later on that? Do not be quick to answer, accept, reject, react, or comment. Timing is the key.

Hyperactivity is moving so quick that sometime, you cause accidents, break things, say the wrong thing and their think, or feel, that you cannot do anything right. If you tend to lack attention to details, then you need to try to focus and listen better.

Parents should love their kids enough to discipline them and reprimand them. Stay focused and lead by example.

Battle Field Readiness prepares us for attacks made by the enemy. In order to defeat and resist the enemy, you have to know that attacks come at your mind, body and spirit as well.

When an attack is imminent, you must be ready to go to battle. Through arenas will vary from time to time, you still must be ready for the element of surprise. When fear overwhelms you, anxious thoughts and emotions will begin to attack your mind. Remember, emotions are not the facts, so deal with the facts, resist and move forward mindfully to defeat the enemy from within and without. "Pray and Strategize before the Good Fight."

The negative energies of a manic-depressive, schizophrenic or deeply depressed individual can drain your energy sometimes; especially if you are constantly trying to motivate them. In fact, sometimes you feel like they are contagious, as well as draining. So we must try to avoid any manipulation by them that may affect or influence our natural high positive, happy, and loving energy. They can really "kill the moment," if you know what I mean. If you have to live or deal with people with these challenges, on a regular basis, learn to manage your feelings and emotions. Set up blockers and strategies, but accept and love them despite their disability.

Beware of non-compliant people who display aggressiveness, hysterical crying, tantrums, and use vile threats of hurting themselves. Take them seriously, but do not let them use these manipulations to control or seduce you to get what they want. Stay strong and be assertive. Do not run away. Beware of people who like to oppose or test or challenge authority, parents, law enforcement, or the legal system. They can be reckless at times. Set some boundaries and defend your emotions and feelings from the start.

VARIOUS LEVELS OF ENERGY WAVES
AND VIBRATIONS

I believe that a light flows through every person, each has a different level of energy power. It is a distinct, individualized clear beam of energy that one day will be revealed or seen in the future. It is invisible to the human eye, but can be observed through scientific techniques as heat ray signatures. In fact, electromagnetic energy can be seen when dynamos produced electricity through the rapid motion of magnets. Wow! What a great force of nature.

There are various forms of waves throughout the universe. We have inventions that were made to control or manipulate microwave noise, radar, and atomic power.

Understanding radar, we have discovered that their waves bump into objects, creates electromagnetic signals or echoes reflected off the object. This was first demonstrated by Hertz sometime in the late 1880's. Also short wave radiation, microwaves, and weather forecasting emerged from these discoveries to eventually include technology like the cell phone and our social network technology. This is what draws me to my conclusion that everything moves, vibrates and has energy. We know that technologic development is surpassing human development. That is why as a Martial Artist, I like Bruce Lee's principal, "Be like water," that is, always be flexible, adapting to change.

My theory of "Individualized Personal Energy" proposed that, despite being invisible to the human eye, one's energy level fluctuates depending on one's thought, emotions, and personal individualized magnetism, as noted in the natural Law of Attraction. One's energy can be affected by many outside forces such as the Moon, the Sun, weather changes, people's will, persons and places, as well as social media.

A person's energy receives its gravitational pull or push from environmental energy known as earth, wind, fire (light or sun light, emotion and soul), water, and the fifth element, iron. However, Faith is your choice, Faith that God has a purpose for you. Individuals who feel the Holy Spirit are "Empowered by a Higher Power."

If you have faith of a mustard seed you can move mountains thereby strengthening your spirit and intellect and maximizing your own God given potential.

Tidal Energy We know the tides are controlled by the moon and the sun. In other words, anything made of water, including the human body, which is approximately three quarters water. Because of this knowledge, we can predict the time of the high or low tides. I caution all to be aware of full moon night's and sudden changes of the weather, because some people are affected and change their behavior and/or character. Also these effects are compounded by drug or alcohol use.

Low Energy people are manipulated by their own internal obsessive thoughts and/or external others who entice or who can dominate, possess and have power over them. Low energy people can be oppressed, manipulated, controlled, dominated and used by higher energy individuals like pawns without them even realizing or, believing it. Usually, lower energy people end up in stagnant or regressed situations in life, making little or no progress and becoming slaves to the mover or controller. Sometimes these individuals give up or quit, as we know. Afterwards, we see health problems of the physical body or the mind. When they give up or quit, they spiritually surrender from the heart. If they do not change their thinking process and reinvent themselves, or self-motivate, the outcome can be catastrophic. The Bible says "As a man/woman thinketh, so is he/she."

The Bible states:

  • Ask and you shall receive
  • Knock and it will be opened
  • Seek and you shall find
  • One must realize that thought waves of your mind can produce positive seeds.

Mind Frame

An "Unbalanced" Mind Can Produce an Unhealthy Mind and Body.

(Q) Do you react emotionally or do you use logic, intellect, tact, and common sense?

(Q) Are you an optimist? Or are you a pessimist?

(Q) Are you free to be or are you controlled or manipulated by others?

(Q) Do you have *"high"* self-esteem or is *"low"* self-esteem holding you down?

(A) Happy thoughts, positive thinking (Cause), promote positive feelings (Effect) and happiness. An ignorant, narrow, or closed mind can promote negative, oppressed, unbalanced thoughts, actions, and reactions.

(Q) What is a slave mentality?

(A) For me, it is those who think they cannot be free, regardless of what they do. They think phrases like: This is how it is, or this is how I am, so maybe might as well accept it. Do you think like that?

Happiness

One's desire to be something gives them a sense of purpose. However, if you have no desire to be something or someone, are you really living or are you just hanging out as kids do?

True joy or happiness does not come from one person or thing. It is a feeling or effect based on many causes or things that make you "feel the moments". It comes from the inner senses within your heart, soul, and mind.

Self-Control Awareness

Do you scream loudly when angered, have tantrums, verbally or physically abuse someone, or hold grudges? Have you taken on some negative traits that you know you should change? For instance, are you rude, scheming, holding grudges, playing games with people (subterfuge), bullying, dominating, controlling, agitating, teasing, instigating, argumentative, slanderous, gossiping, impulsive, hot-headed, treacherous, lying, jealous, fabricating, vile, overly sarcastic, insulting, envious, hateful, always angry, complaining, whining, hyperactive, rebellious, over emotional, easily disturbed, overreacting, exaggerating, undermining, manipulating, vindictive, overly dramatic, wanting to be right all the time, closed minded, non-trusting, or just have a selfish and/or I don't care attitude?

If you constantly display these negative behaviors, it is time to re-evaluate. Do a self-evaluation. Write it down and correct these negative behaviors as soon as possible. Follow up on your list. Of course, there may be more negative habits not mentioned. Remember, only your desire to change can change you. You might also need the assistance of an experienced teacher or mentor. If you remove a negative behavior, replace it with a positive behavior. For instance, replace war with peace, lying with truth, hate with love, and arrogance with humility.

(Q) How do you know if you display these habits?

(A) Ask a good friend, family member, mentor, or let your conscience be your guide. There is nothing sadder than a decent person who is resistant to change or personal progress. There are too many people in the cemetery that probably wished they could have made a difference. Maybe they missed the boat to their dream or destiny, whether by accident or intentionally by giving up. If you don't believe that a cat has nine lives, metaphorically speaking, then know that all of us have more than nine chances to change. So control your negative habits and impulses, develop a plan, write it down and then have Plan B and C if A should fail.

My motto is *"Be a Busy Bee not a lazy turkey."* We can all put our house (self) under construction (enhancing one's attributes). You have heard the universal laws that state, "What goes around, comes around" and "What you put out will eventually come back." Well start thinking about change now, even if it is a 10° turn at a time, as opposed to making a 360° change. Some positive change is better than no change at all. You may need to go into your own cocoon for a little while, a short-term retreat from people, places, and things so you can reemerge as a beautiful, butterfly. Sometimes you have to move out to move up!

Nutrition and Exercise Habits

Understanding the Body's Biological Terrain

By Mark (Wright) Muhammad

In the book, "The Art of War" by Sun Tzu, it states that *understanding the terrain is the highest responsibility of the general; generals who do not know the terrain lose.* The principle of understanding the terrain in warfare is also applicable to understanding your own body's terrain. The human body, in the environment that we live in, is constantly under attack. The enemies are pollutants, toxins from bad food and water, free radical buildup, and ignorance of the knowledge of *life* and how we should *live* it. These enemies are non-personal. They do not discriminate. They take out whatever opponent is in their path.

A *wise* general knows the terrain that is advantageous for his enemy to win. He also knows the terrain that is conducive for him to win to have the advantage. We must look at our bodies in much the same way as a general if we are to win the war against degenerative diseases, aging, and premature death.

In understanding our body's biological terrain, we must first gain knowledge of the terrain and what it encompasses, as well as, the enemies we are fighting. The concept of what is known as *"biological terrain"* describes the environment of our body's living cells. Scientists describe this environment of our bodies by measuring three conditions in the body's fluids:

1)   *Acidity or Alkalinity – pH Level,*

2)   *Antioxidant power or Redox (reduction of oxidation) potential, and*

3)   *Electrical Conductivity*

Acidity and **Alkalinity** are measured by the power (**p**) or amount of hydrogen (**H**). Hydrogen is considered the *fuel of life* because it is used by the Oxygen in our bodies, which actually burns it, thus producing energy from it. As hydrogen increases, the blood and body tissues become less acidic and change to a more desirable alkaline pH. The pH scale ranges from 0 on the acidic end to 14 on the alkaline end. A solution is considered neutral if its pH is 7. The body's blood plasma and other fluids that surround the cells in the body have a pH of 7.2 to 7.3. Scientists discovered that certain bacteria and viruses could only flourish in a very narrow pH range. Most bacteria and viruses flourish in an acidic body environment. Most of the food in our modern diet is too acidic and this produces an imbalance in our bodies. This sets the stage for free radical build-up, which is considered a major cause of aging and some think responsible for 85% of degenerative diseases. We should aim to ingest 80% alkaline foods and 20% acid foods in our diets. In addition to our diets, some other alkalizing conditions are rest, sleep, breathing fresh air, exercise, laughing, conversing, enjoyment, and love.

Oxidation-Reduction Potential (ORP) is another very important factor in good health. The following is an excerpt from an article which explains oxidation-reduction potential (ORP):

Oxidation, which is a regular function of metabolism and cell function, strips an electron from certain molecules. These molecules (called free radicals) then must steal an electron from a nearby molecule to repair themselves, which means that the nearby molecule must steal an electron from another molecule and on and on. This vicious oxidation cycle ends when an electron is taken from a molecule, which has an excess electron to donate. These "donor" molecules are called anti-oxidants and are produced by nature in Vitamin E, Vitamin C, Beta-Carotene, Selenium, etc.

In biological systems, removal or addition of an electron constitutes the most frequent mechanism of oxidation-reduction reactions. These oxidation-reduction reactions are frequently called redox reactions.

Researchers almost universally blame oxidation for premature aging and degenerative diseases. Pollution, chemicals, food additives, pesticides, antibiotics, etc. are thought to dramatically accelerate the oxidation process, increasing the need for anti-oxidants. (Source: http:// www. findhealer.com/mall/telstar/articles/waterfaq.php3).

Research has shown that the most effective anti-oxidants are those that have a redox valve in the range of -200 to -700.

In addition, problems arise when too many free radicals are produced in the body. They attach themselves to normal, healthy cells, such as DNA and RNA, and damage them genetically. This causes many of our cells to be potentially cancerous. Free radicals are produced from air, water and food pollution, sulfites in foods, growth hormones in pork, antibiotics and nitrites in lunchmeats, smoked meats, overheating and frying foods, tobacco smoke, alcohol, prescription drugs, x-rays, asbestos, carcinogens, fertilizers, pesticides and herbicides, chemotherapy, auto exhaust, stress, trauma, and infections.

Electrical Conductivity looks at the body's fluids in terms of its ability to conduct an electrical current. In a universe of thought-wave-vibrations, we are but bodies of transient thought-wave-vibrations. Basically, we are electrical beings. We have the ability to transmit and receive electrical messages on various frequencies depending on the state of our vibratory rate. Our bodies are composed of approximately 70% water and our brains are approximately 90% water. Water without minerals will not conduct electricity. Messages from cells are vital to their functions, but will not be transmitted if minerals are inadequate in the body fluids between and inside the cells. Because our soils and vegetation are often depleted of trace minerals, our body fluids tend to be low in the minerals necessary to transmit vital messages. This can lead to frequent fatigue, poor mental function, and disease. Therefore, electrical conductivity has to be increased in the body fluids.

To find out if your biological terrain is conducive to your winning the war against disease and death, check with your local physician or hospital to see if they are familiar with *Biological Terrain Assessments* (BTA) or *The Metabolic Analysis Test* (MAT). One of the instruments that is capable of testing these three areas of body fluids is called a *Biological Terrain Analyzer*

NOTE: *The information contained in this article is derived from various scientific research data. Comments on this article can be sent to:* **icymaf@yahoo.com**

2013 U.S.A Martial Arts Hall of Fame

Front Row From Left to Right: Anthony Bianciella Esq., Grand Master
Austin Wright Sr., Donald Keith Price and Herman Barnetta
Back Row Middle: Mr. Ken Thompson

CHAPTER 3 – *The System*

THE IDEA OF THE U.W.A. SYSTEM

The history of martial arts dates back well over 2000 years. Various forms of martial arts exist all over the world. The unique style of the U.W.A. system combines martial art forms from Japan, Okinawa, China, and America. All Martial Arts styles have something beneficial to offer, whether traditional, eclectic, or combined M.M.A. styles.

It is well known in the martial arts world that the old masters did not reveal all of their knowledge to their students right away. I believe that this is necessary and with good reason. In order to preserve the traditions of the art, masters keep their best techniques reserved for their most loyal students, those who first prove themselves worthy by exercising good character, respect, and knowledge of Bushido (Way of the Warrior). Most importantly, the Master Instructor should provoke their students to find the answers within themselves.

Most styles of Martial Arts at some point in their history were used for warfare, exercise, security of home and land, hand to hand combat, competition, or self-defense. As for the U.W.A. System, we focus on Ki (inner spirit), discipline, structure, moral principles, etiquette, respect, rules and knowledge of U.W.A.'s "History." This builds a good well-rounded foundation. Defense should come immediately after. Students should know through use of common sense during a hostile situation at what points one would verbalize, check, hurt, maim, or altogether avoid, an adversary. Based on my forty years of experience, I have determined that the U.W.A.'s technique should have strategies and elements of surprise, generated with courage, Ki, Kiai (yell, effort, breathing and force), strong stance (feet, legs, waist, and body posture), visualization and focus.

U.W.A. STRATEGIES

Training throughout the 70's, 80's and 90's consisted of a lot of "lumping and bumping" of students. Students trained without headgear or full sparring safety equipment. This was commonplace in many martial art dojos. Senseis and owners did not worry excessively about being sued because injury was an accepted fact as in any other contact sport. Since 1990, I have felt it necessary to balance physical training with new safety awareness, disciplinary actions, and strict rules, policies, and procedures. My new instructional strategies are designed to enable students to increase their cardio workout, yet limit injuries that could possibly interfere with their daily activities. I incorporated new safety rules, stretching, and warm-up exercises to protect students from injuries which deter beginning students in their early stages of training (Level I) from progression into sport competition and "rank testing." I developed innovative and motivational reflex drills (Self-Defense). Also, I introduced techniques to increase student attention span, self-control, self-discipline, and confidence.

The U.W.A. System nurtures the ability of the student by giving them the opportunity to express themselves through demonstrations of skill and knowledge and class participation. This can be achieved through U.W.A. Forms (Kata) and free style sparring (Kumite), as well as our question and answer period after every class. The younger members of the U.W.A. System present a challenge because of their inquiring minds yet limited attention span. Certified Instructors of the U.W.A. provide stimulating challenges to satisfy student interest. We offer different assault prevention scenarios. For example, would your child know what to do if?

1. He or she got lost in an unfamiliar area?

2. A friendly stranger offers them a ride after school?

3. A person they trust wants to play a "secret" game?

A natural tendency of children is to trust people who appear to be friendly. It is sometimes hard for parents to teach children to balance this trust with caution. We try to provide them with common sense rules that can help keep them aware.

Students are taught discipline. Discipline is training intended to produce a special character pattern of behavior. They are taught how to meditate, focusing on their training and what they are trying to accomplish. We support and encourage all efforts and accomplishments using positive reinforcement even for small successes.

Students are taught best workable solutions to conflicts. In addition, students are taught to never underestimate their opponents. They should always try to be alert. They learn to react instantly to protect their family and self at all times and not to underestimate an attacker. They are instilled with the notion to always fight as if your life depended on it. Students are also taught leadership skills that will assist them in life's many challenges.

Students learn to: Know when and how to defend themselves, family, castle, and principles. Know when and how to be diplomatic. Know when and where to retreat. Know when and how to avoid. Know strategies. Know when and where to attack (choose your battle's time and place). Stay on Point (Guard or Alert). Know the Players. Closely observe people's behavior (eyes, non-verbal gestures and body movements). Students learn to: Know their Opposition and Enemies. Beware of double agents (Chameleons, Saboteurs, Conspirators, and Weak Links). Have instituted Disciplinary Actions and Codes of Conduct. Be prepared for surprise attacks so as to thwart them. Be elusive. Discuss Intervention, prevention, resolution and conflict tactics.

Finally, Students learn to: Have knowledge of Recovery, Spirituality, Support Groups, The Law, Rights, Industry, Competition, and Medicine, "so as to intelligently do what is right despite the predators plan to bring you down..."

Theory of P.A.C.E. 911

Prevention, Intervention, and Defense, U.W.A. Combat Self-Defense Tactics, are designed to deter, stop, or control an adversary. It is important to realize that if you are caught off guard by any attack, the ability to thwart it depends solely on your timing, reflexes, experience, and aggressiveness to regain control and achieve victory over a hostile or threatening situation. For multiple attacks, one should strike and retreat, and exercise common sense. Awareness and street survival skills are very important. Remember that diplomacy and police intervention is your initial line of defense. If you cannot retreat, and an adversary progresses towards you to violate you or cause you bodily harm, use caution in your decision as to how to react.

Competitor Philosophy

Grandmaster Austin Wright, Sr. is the highest ranking authority in the Universal Warrior Arts System. Grandmaster Wright and the Board (Sanctioning Body) will present and validate why Universal Philosophies combined with Martial Arts Styles can prove successful in the education of "self-defense," "sport competition" and "physical exercise."

What works for one student may or may not work well for another, depending on size, strength, speed, flexibility, coordination, endurance and age. Go with what works at the time. Bounce between old traditional styles and new eclectic styles, thus evolving daily in your training. Do not be narrow minded.

Authentic technique can only be taught by certified, professional, and qualified instructors who can teach the forms, basics, and give honest and thorough explanations of the moves (Bunkai).

U.W.A. Form is an artistic war dance or "way" of expressing our eclectic traditional Wright Family Lineage. It demonstrates history, confidence, attitude, stance, techniques, determination, evolution, strength, and knowledge of the "Art."

Rules of Engagement

The first rule of sparring is "Do not let anger overwhelm you." Stay focused on your strategies and techniques, yet be aggressive and appear relaxed. If you become "angry," sublimate (transform) that energy into a positive motivating force. Like high-test fuel for an engine, use anger constructively for your advantage, not destructively. As I always say, "I don't get mad, I get stronger, especially when I defend my rights and my principles!" If you control your emotions you have truly develop Self-Control. Later Self-Control will be seen in your Actions and Character.

Sport Competition Pointers

- Strategize, get set and go, or wait, depending on whether you are an offensive, defensive, or dual warrior.

- Perfect one technique first.

- Adapt and improvise against an opponent who is your equal or better. Beat them at the waiting and timing game.

- Always fight fast, hard, and without notice. Remember, protect yourself at all times.

- At the beginning and end of the "sport" competition, display a positive attitude and acknowledge the winners. Recall who you lost to and how you lost.

- Love what you do, train hard, then train some more.

Being a former competitor, I can appreciate talent in forms and fighting. It is important, however for the "New Age Warrior" to ask potential warriors (sport competitors) to show their true intentions and make a pledge. Thus, the U.W.A. System Self-Defense Karate Academy/Universal Dojo, the Board Members and I shall not teach our "best" sport/Martial Arts techniques (AKA Trade Secrets) to advanced students (Brown/Black Belts) unless they sign a pledge of allegiance (loyalty) and non-competition agreement.

Sport Free Style Karate Safety Sparring Rules

I.   Safety equipment is recommended (i.e., headgear, mouthpiece, groin protector, footpads, shin pads, hand pads)

II.   Controlled sparring as per semi-contact U.W.A. rules.

III.   No contact to the face or vital areas.

IV.   Target Areas – **Legal Targets:** front of body (torso), ribs, side of head gear, and leg checks. **Illegal Targets:** front of face, back of head, back of body, and groin area (below the belt in general).

V.   Rules of discipline and respect shall be practiced at all times toward students, instructors, coaches, and referees.

VI.   Disrespect, lack of self-control, excessive contact, unsportsmanlike behavior, will not be tolerated.

VII.   **Note:** These safety rules protect all. At no time shall these rules be broken. If students do not comply with these rules, they will be disciplined and/or dismissed from the arena/Dojo.

Understanding Mind & Body

Develop Your Own Personalized Survival Skills

The U.W.A. System is beneficial in all aspects of human life.

Psychologically: Positive Karma/Energy, Optimism, and Self-Control

Physically: Exercise, Health, and Nutrition

Spiritually: Meditation, Self-Awareness, and Inner Strength

Practically: Builds Confidence, Skills, and Maturity

Students must learn how not to let their emotions override their intellect. Panic can cause negative outcomes or uncontrolled outbursts. Since emotions effect reactions, one must learn to control them. One must be emotionally mature. This is a constant battle within oneself (e.g., old nature vs. new nature). Emotionally mature means being aware of feelings and controlling your impulsiveness, or responding before thinking. One can sublimate hyperactivity, frustrations and/or excess energies (positive or negative Karma/Energy) through supervised, disciplined and controlled training applications. This requires a commitment to evolve one's thinking and discipline. The best way to handle feelings (negative or positive) is to be aware of them, admit that they exist (in reality), than express them honestly and clearly. We all need to develop an individual defense mechanism, which can be utilized responsibly. Develop a positive way to avoid unpleasant, threatening, or irritating emotions. Students must develop their own personalized survival skills.

Stress causes one to feel a sense of imbalance.

Tension is emotional stress which makes students feel sad, angry, worried, tired, and nervous. There is positive and negative stress, for instance, testing times, schedule times, pressures in taking tests, not being prepared, etc.

There are everyday pressures of life such as maintaining financial stability or emotional stability. It is important that we understand conflict (war) and resolution (peace). Unresolved iniquities (negative past actions) of wrongdoings must be resolved or put to closure so that one experiences positive self-esteem and pride. Students must develop, through trial and error, strategies to deal with different struggles throughout their lives. Family, friends, positive role models, reading, doctors, therapists, should be readily available as support systems based on what works best for you. When possible, try to present or articulate your point of view through calm deliberation and tact. Keep in mind people's feelings when reprimanding and disciplining others. Be alert to those who like to provoke you, such as agitators or instigators.

The body readies you through your five senses (awareness) and the sixth sense, "gut feeling" or intuition. Beware of the element of surprise. When you sense "danger," adrenaline runs through the body. It prepares you to be stronger, faster, and your five senses become hyper-vigilant. One must be aware that adrenaline is the body's "natural" defense mechanism. It can make your stomach feel like "butterflies," or sap your energy, if it continues for a long period of time (mental/physical exhaustion). However, its main purpose is defense or combat readiness of the human body for "fight or flight."

Beware of the "freeze mode." The "freeze mode" is when one does not react. That is to say, you mentally know what to do, however, your mind and body are not as one at that particular moment. For instance, when someone tells you their intentions, such as to striking you, and you do not move, block or counter strike. Instead you stay there and get hit. This is a form of "freeze mode".

With the approval of a physician, children and adults can train in Martial Arts. Usually Martial Arts increase one's attention span, one's focus (concentration), and one's self-control. Awareness and self-discipline can control acts of aggression or outbursts (tantrums). Constant training builds confidence and reduces stress levels, thereby promoting a healthy mind and body. This helps enhance one's character and can develop a positive individual, who can contribute positively to our socio/economic community.

Martial Art students need to develop ways to protect their mind as well as their body. These methods are called **Defense Mechanisms**. Three positive ways to help you channel excess energy are:

1. **Sublimation** – taking one's excess energy and placing it into a positive interaction, i.e., dance, sports, and art.
2. **Compensation** – If you're not good in "sports," focus more on Kata, weapons, or history.
3. **Humor** – Be able to have a sense of humor about minor negative events and be optimistic in general.

"Recovery from traumatic experiences (physical or emotional) is the key to "moving on…"

Most people should try to avoid "unworthy altercations." Arguments or disagreements can cause inter-personal conflicts. If inter - personal conflicts are not resolved, or dismissed, it can cause some irreconcilable differences. Remember, a lot of how you think, act, and respond, depends on your attitude, life experience, training and degree of self-control. Much of my knowledge and understanding of the mind and body came from personal experiences and studies while working in a psychiatric unit for several years at Bayonne Hospital. I have also worked with emotionally challenged children and adolescents in the private/public special education school system in Hudson County, New Jersey since 1999.

VARIOUS FORMS OF ADDICTION

If you are promiscuous and a part of you is out of control, then your social and sexual energy lacks discipline. When you make up reasons why, or rationalize that it is okay to have sex with anyone, because you feel you are not hurting anyone (yet), that should be the first sign of denial. If you realize that you are continuing this self-destructive behavior, you should first admit to creating the problem, then begin to manage it! Do something about it. Seek professional help or try to take control of it, by developing Self-Control. In the long term, Hearts get broken and cheating causes divorces and break ups which means you are not ready to settle down or be in a responsible relationship or marriage.

Addictions come in various forms: Gambling, Hustling, Promiscuity, Smoking, Alcoholism, Drug Addicts, Adrenaline Junkies and Over Eating are all forms of addiction. Legal drug addictions include caffeine, alcohol, prescriptions, and cigarettes with nicotine.

When an individual is addicted, they are in a state of denial. They rationalize everything related to their habit of choice, including believing that they are in control of their addiction and that they can stop at any time that they choose. However, at this point, they do not want to stop the sex, alcohol or drug use because, first, they resist change naturally. And second, they are not really ready to stop. They like it. It is a part of their corrupted mind, body, and spirit. They have accepted and not rejected it as foreign and hurtful to them. It has become pleasurable in most cases and the euphoria provides a false sense of security. Sadly it is a nice high for the short term but the long term will mean suffering and pain. In some cases, their addiction will end in, stroke, heart attack, HIV, hepatitis, prison and death.

A drug overdose can cause "Black Outs" or loss of memory. Sometimes it includes, paranoid delusions, when the addict begins to see and hear things that are not actually happening. They hallucinate. One time, I heard an addict say "that he heard the Devil talking to him, saying all money was evil….." But it was not money. It was his addiction and how he used his rent money to buy his drugs. Not taking responsibility for his poor choice. Deciding to pay rent versus spending it all on the drugs.

I highly recommend, kids and teens, "Do not get involved in drug trafficking, selling dope or pushing drugs for quick money. First, you will eventually get caught by the police or killed by a "customer" or the competition. Second, you are slowly killing yourself, your friends and fellow human beings. Yes, you are right, someone else will do it despite the consequences, but it does not mean it has to be you!

If you are in the drug game and are still alive, reading this, you have options. First, a choice, get out of the game while you have a choice. Move away! Tell your buddies you are going away. Don't tell them why or where. Just find a friend, relative, or sibling to hold you up, until you get your life in order. But do not continue the game or hustle. You are better than that! But you need to believe that and feel this.

Remember there are cameras everywhere, especially on the street corners. Also there are rats, haters, snitchers, addicts, and your own competition that will eventually sell you out. There is no love or trust in this game. Only short term money, losers, pawns, players, prisoners, and the walking dead, or what I like to call Zombies. Zombies are not people who eat flesh, but they are drug recipients or receivers, who are out of control, and some have a death wish. They will take you with them, so beware.

Prescription addicts are up and coming on a large scale. Prescription pills are now sold on the street corners for profit, stolen from pharmacies or family members. Some people even sell their personal narcotic pills to a dealer, who then turns around and to make his profit, reselling it at a higher price.

We are Every Day Heroes Taking Responsibility

Some people feel like they have a *"thorn in their side," "a monkey on their back."* If you can't control a bad habit or remove it, then learn to "manage it." Remember the Serenity Prayer:

"God grant me the serenity to accept the things I cannot change; Courage to change the things I can; and wisdom to know the difference" (Theologian Reinhold Niebuhr).

There are some recovering alcoholics and drug addicts who realize that the next drink or taste of drugs will send them immediately back to the enslavement of the alcohol or drug of choice. However, despite knowing the truth or facts, they tend to back slide. The addiction is a thorn in their side and affects their mind, body, spirit, and emotional well-being. However, they must learn to "manage it".

As addicts begin to manage their vices, they regain their emotional and financial stability. However, recovery time is needed. National and State AA (Alcoholics Anonymous) and NA (Narcotics Anonymous) programs are available to encourage and assist addicts through the tough times.

Verbal Ju-Jitsu

You must develop self-defense strategies for verbal attacks. Bullies know how to bait and provoke. Their lifestyle is to engage, but we must resist and defeat the enemy with practical strategies. In order to defeat the enemy, you must first learn how to resist.

Kids can be mean and belligerent when it comes to making threats or teasing. Verbal Ju-Jitsu is needed to defend yourself from the start! Sometimes it is harmless and horse play, sometimes it is serious. Here is a hypothetical scenario.

Let's imagine visualize someone threatens you to test your courage, pretend it is a schoolmate, someone you know, or a team mate. They say, "I will get you afterschool! If you don't do what I tell you to do." Flip or spin around their verbal assault and redirect them if you can, but do not show signs of fear or nervousness. You can reply or say, what are you going to do? Beat me up? That's a threat! Well, I guess I will have to tell someone or secretly tell someone. Which will usually get them to change their minds and it's over. But sometimes this can provoke a bully. If you do not have physical self-defense skills, be careful not to engage the bully, instead, make a scene to alert others around you, warn the bully leave me alone." I will press charges, tell the teacher, Mom or Dad.

Even if nothing happens to you, still report it, or tell your friends, family member, Mom, Dad, or local authorities. If it occurs in school, tell teachers or the principal. If it is on the street or in the park, get to safety ASAP. Call 911 and make a police report for documentation purposes.

If you are threatened on the street while walking to your car, school, or home, you might have to run or walk away quickly, not taking your eyes off the perpetrator (see my Seven Street Survival Commandments). Also remember what they are wearing, hair and eye color, speech, language, and body language, look for scars, to report and apprehend the perpetrator.

Beware of anyone who is mean, belligerent, vile, hostile, manipulative and arrogant. You know them by their company and they make you feel uncomfortable in their presence. They are dangerous and bad company.

We cannot control people's actions or words, but we can control how we react to it. When attack is imminent, however, action is needed. When engaged by someone by a verbal attack, instead of a physical confrontation, redirect and parry their negativity. Don't absorb the verbal abuse, learn to "Roll with the Punches" and just walk away Twart the Lure.

ABOUT YOUR SOUL, PURPOSE AND IDENTITY

Your soul is your true identity or personality. It is who we really are on the inside. In society or public, we have many masks that we wear that veil our true identity don't we? What is your purpose or goal in life? What is your passion? What are you naturally good at? You must discover your purpose. Don't let anyone else choose for you. Once you discover who you are, then you will know where you are going and join with others that share similar goals in life. Remember, the life and legacy that you leave, is how you will be remembered. How do you want to do remembered prior to physically departing this world?

UWA Martial Arts Testing Manual

Universal Dojos?

(Q) Why is diversity important in Dojos?

(A) Diversity is a pattern emerging steadily in most Dojos in the new millennium. Diversity brings about open-mindedness and enables all to learn from other cultures.

(Q) What causes problems for local Dojos?

(A) Economic rivalry, prejudices, adversity, lack of integrity, egos, jealousy, vanity, slander, false pride, fear of change, and difference in opinions. This is often the root cause of dissention in some Dojos. I believe most styles are good, however, it's really up to the students and leaders to keep a style alive.

"United, all Martial Artists can stand together, grow and prosper"

U.W.A. Basic Exercises – Upper Body –

Self-Defense Techniques

I. Most upper body exercises start with a ◁▷ Pyramid Stance.

II. All upper body techniques start at chest level for form purposes and timing.

III. (ROS) means repeat opposite side, (R) means right (L) means left.

1. Step forward with the right foot into Toe to Heel Stance. Vertical Punch right – Vertical Punch left. Repeat opposite side. (ROS).

2. Step forward with the right foot into Toe to Heel Stance. Upper cut right - Upper Cut left. ROS.

3. Step forward with the right foot into Toe to Heel Stance. Corkscrew punch left - Corkscrew Punch right. ROS.

4. Step forward with the right foot into Toe to Heel Stance. Lion Claw Strike (L) & (R) hand. ROS.

5. Step back with the right foot into Toe to Heel Stance. Left open hand downward Shuto Block. Vertical Punch right- Punch left. ROS.

6. Step back with the right foot into Toe to Heel Stance. Left hand closed fist inside Hammer Fist Block. Vertical Punch right Punch left. ROS.

7. Step back with the right foot into Toe to Heel Stance. Left hand shoulder high Shuto Block. Horizontal Fingertip Stab to the throat with the right hand, then with the left. ROS.

8. Step forward with the right foot into Toe to Heel Stance. Rising Shuto Jam Block with the right hand. Hammer Fist left hand to face. ROS.

9. Step forward with the right foot into Toe to Heel Stance. Closed-fist right Forearm Block, step forward with left foot, left hand Wrist Grab, then step with right foot forward and perform a right hand Hook Grab for take down with (R) foot forward and/or disarm (3 steps total). ROS.

10. Step back with the right foot into Toe to Heel Stance. Raise left open hand to cover the left side of your ear, with a Vertical Elbow Strike then followed by a Horizontal Elbow Strike to the bridge of the nose. ROS.

11. Step back with the right foot into a Horse Stance.   Left hand open Downward Hook Block, step back with (L) foot, (R) hand open Downward Hook Block.   Right Closed Fist Guard, reverse left Corkscrew Strike. ROS.

12. (R) Closed Fist Guard from an Angle Stance, (R) Back Hand fake, then a Back Hand Jam, take down (trap), then a left Reverse Horizontal Punch. ROS.

13. Closed Fist Right Guard from an Angle Stance, (R) foot forward, back hand fake, step (L) foot forward crossed behind and in front of the (R) foot, spin (L) 360° followed by a spinning (L) hand Shuto to opponent's opening and ending in the opposite (L) Angle Guard Stance. ROS.

14. Step forward (R) foot into (R) Angle Horse Stance, (R) hand downward Parry Block followed by a left Ridge Hand to the upper body. ROS.

15. Step back (R) foot into Toe to Heel Stance. Double Shuto Block Grab, (L) hand high Parry Circular Cross Arm Trap, shove (R) Lion Claw to face and (L) Inverted Heel Hand Strike to groin. ROS.

All exercises were developed by Grandmaster Austin Wright, Sr. for self-defense and practical application purposes.

U.W.A. Kicks

1. Straight forward thrust/snap kick

2. Side snap kick

3. Side thrust kick

4. Jumping side thrust/snap kick

5. Knee strike

6. Crossover stomp

7. Muay Tai kick

8. Crescent kick

9. Spinning back kick

10. Whirl wind kick

11. Wind kick

12. Hook kick

13. Ax kick

14. Scissors kick

15. Shin jam

16. Back kick

Wright's Universal Dojo of
Self-Defense Martial Arts Academy

RULES AND PROCEDURES -AGREEMENT

The following rules and procedures are a mandatory requirement. Intentional defiance of these rules will result in disciplinary action to include loss of membership and/or loss of certification/rank recognition.

1. No shoes are to be worn on dojo floor.

2. No gum chewing in class and no leaning on walls.

3. Students are to always train in a clean and ironed uniform.

4. Students should make it a point to arrive ten minutes early for each class.

5. A student cannot leave class without permission.

6. Students are not to give a public demonstration of Martial Arts without their   instructors' permission or bring issues to the dojo for settling.

7. You must have approval of your instructor before competing in a tournament.

8. Any substitute teacher will be treated as your regular Sensei.

9. A respectful bow is to be given whenever going on or off the training floor.

10. Students are to stand at attention whenever an instructor is talking or showing a technique unless otherwise stated by the instructor.

11. Students are to maintain an attendance of no less than two classes per week.

12. Students are to sign in for each class they attend.

13. Line-up by rank when class is called to start.

14. After bowing onto the floor for the first time, students should then go to the photo of the Wrights and bow to show respect.

15. It is up to everyone to help keep the Dojo spotless by cleaning-up after every class. Also students should inquire from time to time to see if any help is needed with demonstrations, tournaments, teaching, etc.

16. Students are encouraged to ask questions and they may do so during class at the appropriate time without interrupting the instructor.

17. If a student must withdraw from the dojo temporarily or permanently, he or she must courteously do so by letting the head instructor know in person or writing a letter. Upon withdrawal from the Dojo, you must give written notice dated 15 days before you leave. Failure to do so could result in loss of membership and belt ranks.

18. To promote safety, no student should be allowed to spar without basic equipment such as a protective cup (males only) and mouthpiece. Additional protective gear such as shin and instep protectors, safety boots, headgear and safety punch are highly recommended (Chest protectors & sports bras for ladies).

19. Students who arrive late for class are to stand at attention at the edge of the dojo floor until the instructor gives them permission to join the class.

20. Inside the Dojo, no form of disrespectful, defiant, disruptive, inappropriate or rude behavior will be tolerated, and will be dealt with as

soon as possible.

21. Board members will hold a meeting for students who violate these rules and procedures to discuss continuing membership eligibility.

22. It is a privilege and an honor to be on a National Team. So let's keep up the good work.

23. Let us all be safety conscience when sparring or using self-defense techniques (see sparring rules).

24. All Instructors/Teachers shall perform, have knowledge of, and demonstrate U.W.A. Federation's Black Belt "Code of Conduct" (signed contract) at all times. Any form of defiance of the "Codes and/or Rules" shall require disciplinary action and a meeting of the Board Members. The President of the U.W.A. Federation™ shall have the "Final Say!"

Wright's Universal Dojo of Self-Defense
Universal Warrior Arts (U.W.A.) Academy

U.W.A. Federation of America ™

Pronunciation of Japanese Vowels

A = AH		U	= OOH
I = EE		AI	= I
E = EH		Y	= I
O = OH		YU	= EEU

UWA Vocabulary and Terminology

Hanshi A. Wright Sr.	Founder & Director of the U.W.A. System
U.W.A.	"The All Changing Warrior"
Soke	Founder & Highest Authority
Karate	"Empty Hand"
Judo	"Gentle Way"
Balance	"Level," Yin-Yang
Rei	Bow
Sensei	Teacher
Shihan	Master Instructor
Osu	Acknowledgement/Respect
Gi	Karate Uniform
Obi	Belt
Kumite	Sparring Match
Testing	Knowledge & Ability
Universal	For All

Kyu	Brown Belt & Below
Sai	Okinawan 3 Prong Sword
Nukite	Finger Tip Strike
Bunkai	Explanation of Move
Ki	Inner Spirit
Dojo	Martial Arts Gym
Suratte	Sit
Kick-boxing	Combination of Kicks and Punches
Kata	Form
Osh	Respect
Dan/Degree	Black Belts
Kung Fu	To Have Skills"
Karate Ka	Student of Karate
Kime	Focus
Kodokan	"School of Studying the Judo Way"
Kiai	Yell
Maki Wara	Striking Board
Yame	Stop/Line up Quietly
Hajame	Begin
Bo	Wooden Staff 6ft.
Jo	Wooden Staff 4ft.
Sword	Long Blade
Empi	Elbow Strike
Jujutsu	"The Compliant Art"
Bushido	"Way of the Warrior"

Japanese Counting

Ichi	One
Ni	Two
San	Three
Shi	Four
Go	Five
Roku	Six
Shichi	Seven
Hachi	Eight
Ku	Nine
Ju	Ten
Ju Ichi	Eleven
Ju Ni	Twelve
Ju San	Thirteen
Ni Ju	Twenty
Ni Ju Ichi	Twenty-one
San Ju	Thirty
Yon Ju	Forty
Go Ju	Fifty

"A man, who has attained mastery of an art, reveals it in his every action."

- Samuri Maxim

Forms And Origins

Here are the Martial Art Forms and Origins, which are the makeup of the U.W.A. System. You must first understand the definition of these styles so as to broaden your knowledge.

Karate – is a style of empty hand. It utilizes movements such as, blocks, thrust, snaps, kicks and hand strikes (Hard style). The use of elbows and knee strikes is for close quarter combat self-defense. This knowledge comes from Okinawa, Japan, and Korea (Tae Kwon Do).

Kung-Fu – is a graceful style. A general name or style of which uses slow, fast and springy movements of techniques and exercises (soft & hard style). This knowledge comes from China.

Jujutsu – is the method of maiming, grappling, and controlling the body parts to stop a hostile adversary. It is used for modern warfare. This style is from Japan.

Judo – means the "gentle way". It was designed to turn an attacker's strength against him. "Sport" form of throws, sweeps. Rolls, and reaps. This style originated in Tokyo, Japan.

American Kickboxing – is a combination of American Boxing and several different Karate kicks for sport full contact purposes/Cardio-kickboxing workout.

Universal Judo-Jujutsu Concepts

<u>**Atewaza**</u> – The art of attacking vital points.

<u>**Head**</u> – top point for head butts.

<u>**Ude**</u> – (The Arm) fingertips, fist, heel, knuckles, elbow, and inner and outer blade of hand (ridge/Shuto).

<u>**Ashi**</u> – (The Leg) Knee cap, ball of foot, and heel.

<u>**Vital Points**</u> – Eyes, ears, nose, neck, jaw, solar plexus, ribs, kidneys, groin, knee, elbow, and joints.

<u>**Nagewaza**</u> – the art of throwing, includes various throws, sweeps, reaps from standing positions and lying positions.

<u>**Katamewaza**</u> – the art of grappling, includes various floor fighting and maiming body parts. Such as, holding, choking, bending, and twisting joints.

Universal Dojo's Judo-Jujutsu Exercises

1. Meditation

2. Stretching

3. Conditioning (Jump Rope, Running, Jumping Jacks)

4. Calisthenics (Push-ups, Sit ups)

5. Wrist Flex   (Inner/Outer)

6. Fingertip Push-ups (5,4,3,2,1 fingers)

7. Squats

8. Heel Raisers

9. Lying on back extend legs overhead (stretch)

10. Pyramid Push-ups (Builds neck muscles)

11. Blowfish (Defense from chokes)

12. Toe-to-Heel Pivots (Left/Right palms facing up)

13. Vital Points (Knowledge of striking areas: eyes, ears, throat, groin, armpit, nose, knees, side & back of neck)

14. Loosening Up Techniques (Slap/Grab/Strike groin; Strike/Jab to throat, eyes)

15. Rolls, Falls, Throws, Reaps, Sweeps, Locks and Strikes

16. Seven Street Commandments of Street Survival (see table of contents)

Judo-Jujutsu Forms

The U.W.A. system utilizes "Sport" Forms of Judo and the Jujutsu Forms for Self-Defense. Meditation, conditioning exercises (warm ups) and stretching are essential prior to this type of training.

Break falls, rolls, and knowledge of breaking one's balance and getting good low wide stances for power techniques are recommended.

- Drawing, ankle throw (Tsuri-Komi-Ashi)
- Wrist manipulations
- Major outer reaping (O-Suto-Gari)
- Neck lock from rear
- Major hip throw (O-Goshi)
- Bent elbow take down
- Shoulder holding (Kata-Gatame)
- Straight arm take down
- Cross arm lock (Juji Gatame)
- Inner reaping (Ouchi-Gari)
- Shoulder throw (Seui-Nage)
- Free-style matches (Randori)

Understand formulas for countering all moves (e.g. Defenders can fall on their back, throw over to the side or use the one-foot throw).

Write essays on the principle of Balance and Excessive Force.

Write essays on Emotions and Self-Control.

Write essays on Logic, Common Sense, and Intuition (gut instinct or 6th sense).

The Wright's Form Repertories

The Wright Pyramid Stance (Self-Defense)
My Entire Classical Wright Repertoire

The Wright Beginners Kata Repertoire

(Developed by Grandmaster Dennis A. Wright, Sr.)

The Wright Earth Kata Repertoire

The Wright Wind Kata Repertoire

The Wright Water Kata Repertoire

The Wright Fire Kata Repertoire

The Iron Kata

Universal Warrior Arts translated means *"The All Changing Warrior"*

We also utilized universal stances and kicks for "sport" competition. A certified Instructor shall have a copyrighted certification rank certificate, Soke stamp, and Universal Dojo of Self Defense, Inc. seal of approval. Also a U.W.A. Martial Arts Federation of America student number and registration number. The Universal Dojo of Self-Defense, Inc., main headquarters is registration #0001, (AKA the Main Headquarters of the U.W.A. Martial Arts Federation of America). All charters shall be given with a certificate of approval. Society Hill I is registration #0002, and Jersey City Karate League is registration #0003, and the Girl Scouts of America Karate League, #0004.

U.W.A. Knowledge of Balance, Air and Force

I. **Students should have their Doctor's approval before participating in any physical "sports" activities.** Proper breathing, stretching, and relaxation were taught to Grandmaster Wright while working as a physical therapist assistant, Combat Medic (U.S. Air Force), during training in Kung-Fu, and by teacher Master Dennis A. Wright Sr.

II. Students are first taught how to relax and control their breathing and nervous energy during meditation. Later, this breathing technique is applied to all of the Air and Force principles of the U.W.A. concepts.

III. The proper inhaling and exhaling of air ($O2$ and $CO2$ exchange) and application of Force (effort) concepts are important.

IV. The Air and Force chart is explained to all new students. Also the proper foundation of forms, stances, chambering kicks, curling toes, clenching hands, balance, posture, eye contact, vital points, and theory is taught with practicality.

V. Student "self-evaluation" and knowledge of U.W.A.'s concepts are discussed. Knowledge of meditation, visualization, strategies, balance, guards, focus, efforts, air, forces, targets, kiai, defense/offense, mind, body, and Ki (as one), recovery, and discipline are studied for understanding.

The U.W.A. System of Air (Breathing) and Force (Technique) Chart

I.   U.W.A. Taikyoku and Earth Forms provide balance, breath control, meditation, and explosive forces.

II.   Spinning and speed techniques are found in Wind Kata, Fire Kata, and Basic Self-Defense strikes and maneuvers (#1 to 15 and kicks).

III.   Our balance, rolls, and break fall principles come from past knowledge of Judo and JuJutsu, and Karate principles.

IV.   Bouncing, faking, footwork, and jumping techniques can be found in Water Kata and Basic Exercises.

V.   Stance foundations are practiced in Forms and Basic Exercise Drills and a lower stance provides a better center of gravity.

VI.   Self-Control is the key to newfound power.

VII.   "Repetition" of Forces (Techniques) and "Awareness" of Air (Proper Breathing) develop skills. Skills make one's techniques (strikes, blocks, kicks, parries, ducks, throws, maiming, sweeps, reaps, etc.) or Combined Forces look more natural and fluid…You must apply on the mechanical (Basic Exercises) and non-mechanical (ducking, leaning, feinting, etc.) in combination during a "sparring" match. You should try to master one technique at a given time. In this way one becomes a technician in the competition arena.

Universal Warrior Art's® Seven Commandments of Street Survival

1. Don't underestimate anybody! Be on alert (readiness) at all times!

2. Don't show off! Strike hard. Strike fast and strike suddenly! Observe people's behaviors (actions) and take notice to your own gut feelings.

3. Learn to react instantly and use **P.A.C.E.** 911.

4. Don't hesitate to use such techniques as hair pulling, eye gouging, or other means to assist you (street fighting). Know the Law (National, State, and Local).

5. After attacking or counter attacking, don't lose sight of your adversary. Be alert for a continuation of an adversary's attack.

6. Know the vital areas and yell (kiai) while delivering "your" best self-defense techniques to deter an attacker.

7. Always fight aggressively and protect yourself at all times. Remember Wright's Universal Dojo's Golden Rule – Caution (verbally) prior to Combat (hurt), Combat prior to Maim (incapacitate), Maim prior to annihilation. For all life is precious.

P.A.C.E. 911

P. = Prevention/Intervention (Have a plan and develop a drill, for instance like a fire drill). Be Alert!

A. = Assess the situation. Improvise when necessary. Remember peace before war.

C. = Calm the situation. Do not panic (resolution) under siege. First you must think and react (or vice versa), control the situation or get help! And/or flee to safety (depending on the scenario).

E. = Evaluate, record and document facts. Call 911.

If you must fight or defend your family, use only the amount of force necessary to deter your attacker(s). Know your rights and don't be ignorant of the law.

Self-Defense Tactical Techniques:

Note: All self-defense techniques start out with the pyramid stance if possible and remember P.A.C.E. 911. Self-defense works with readiness and continual training.

BLOCKS

Vertical Punch

Uppercut

Cork Screw Punch

Lion Claw Strike

<u>Downward Shuto (Chop) Block</u>

Hammer Fist Block

Position 1

Hammer Fist Block Inside

Position 2

<u>Execution of Inside Hammer Fist Block</u>

Position 3

Shoulder High Shuto Block
Position 1

Fingertip Strike

Rising Shuto Block

Left Guard Position

Forearm Block

X Block

Vertical Elbow Strike

Horizontal Elbow Strike

Execution of Elbow Strike

One Person Attacker:

1. Push: (One Hand) Push-Pull – Step back, Wrist Grab,
Strike to throat and Judo Throw. (Two Hand) Push-Pull/Counter Attack.

Arm Wrap

Elbow Strike to Face Throw

Ogoshi

Hip Throw

Take Down Heel Stomp

Turn Over Arm Control

2. Choke (Utilize Blowfish): (Two-Hand) Frontal choke-Interlock Hands and step away, Elbow Downward Rake. Counter with Elbow to face, Knee, or Football Kick to groin area. (Two Hand Rear choke) – One Arm Swing around Strike-two. Hand Push and Reap forward leg.

Step 1

2

3

Top Left – 1

Top Right - 2

Bottom Left - 3

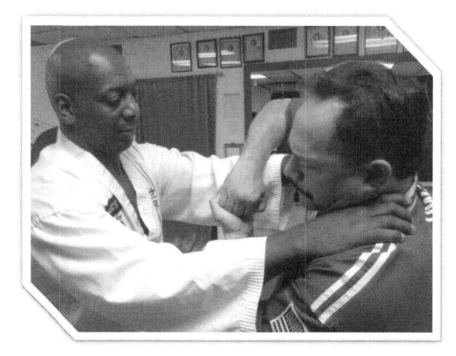

Interlock Hands - 1

Break Hold - 2

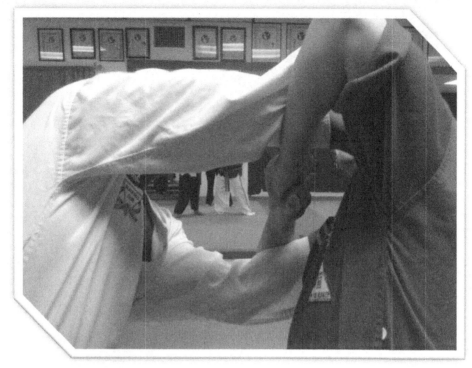

Interlock Hands – side views

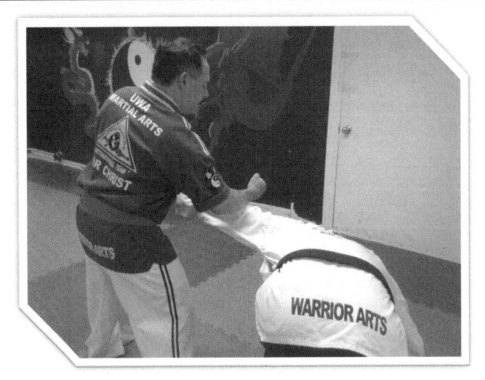

One Arm Elbow Break

3. Bear Hug Hold: (Frontal Hold) Use a Head Butt Attack – Pyramid, open arms Ogoshi. Judo Throw, Foot Stomp, Counter Strike. (Rear Hold) Drop low and perform an Ankle Lift (Jujutsu), Falling Elbow and Roll.

4. Lapel Grab: (One-Arm Hold) Push-Pull – Strike outside Elbow, Inside Elbow, rising #8 block, ridge to groin. (Two Arm Hold) Two hand bell slap to ears, head butt to nose and #10 exercise.

5. Wrist Grab: (One Arm Pull-Push) front leg Sweep and Counter Strike, Stomp. (Two Arm) #15 (Before) (After) Knee Strike to groin and Counter Hand Strike.

6. Sucker Round Punch: Spear Block, Elbow to face, and Osuto Gari (outside reap) or Knee Strike.

7. Jab: Parry, Duck, followed up by a low Side Thrust Kick to the knee or Back Kick to the groin area.

8. Bat or Stick: When possible, Jam swinging hand by Arm Lock, disarm attacker and Take Down (subdue, control, or maim). **Rule:** Expect to take a partial hit when stepping forward to stop weapons.

9. Knife: Overhead attack-step to the outside of the attacker, Parry or Block. Disarm attacker and take down (subdue, control, or maim). **Rule:** Expect to get possible lacerations and have knowledge of knives.

10. Gun: In close quarter combat only – instructions for advanced level students only. To be taught only by Former Veterans of Armed Forces, to include knowledge and use of a firearm.

The U.W.A. Patch®

Through my knowledge, experience, as well as the critique and evaluation of *Bunkai* (explanation of the moves) angles, timing, and spacing, I developed the five elements of *Kata* (forms) known as: **Earth, Wind, Fire, Water** *and* **Iron.** These Kata concepts were developed for educational, practical, sport, and combative arts purposes. They are combined with Universal principles and scientific concepts. To visualize the ideals of this system, I (Grandmaster Wright) designed the U.W.A. Federation Patch with the assistance of my chief instructor, Sensei Antonio Wilson.

The Inspiration for the Patch

One spring day (1997), Hanshi Austin Wright, Sr. was training privately in the Hudson County Park in Bayonne, New Jersey, with his son (Austin Jr.). Hanshi Wright pondered and meditated on the techniques and ideas to be pursued in the development of his eclectic system.

"The park was serene and colorful, due to the beautiful leaves and flowers budding and blooming. There was a light breeze that flowed through the air. I sent my son to practice some tournament techniques and sat down quietly on the grass after a five-mile run to meditate on what moves I should incorporate into my forms. Next, I needed to enhance my logo design to create a new U.W.A. Martial Arts Federation patch. Suddenly I was drawn to what appeared to be a dust devil (a miniature weak tornado). While studying this natural phenomenon, I noticed how the wind whisked up some leaves dirt and twigs and spun them swiftly in a circle. I also noticed the way the leaves, dirt and twigs were spread out at an angle and thrust back onto the grass. Interesting, I thought.

These will be my concepts, natural forces like spinning techniques, angle techniques, fast and slow forces and elements of surprise...Hence, Earth, Wind, Fire, Water, and Iron Forms (Katas) were created and the new concept of the patch was born (see U.W.A. Patch)."

The Meaning of the Patch

The U.W.A. Federation patch represents the training of the mind, body, and spirit. The pyramid, an ancient and powerful symbol (Triad), represents the Mind, Body, & Spirit. The Yin/Yang symbol, which is an age-old universal concept, represents balance. Complimentary to each other are the clenched fist on the right, which represents war, and the open hand on the left, which represents peace. The Chinese Dragon represents Wisdom, Power, and Good Fortune. The *Kanji* (Japanese writing) on the U.W.A. patch represents the elements of Earth, Wind (Air), Fire, Water, and Iron (self-awareness). The Black Background represents the Universe/Infinity. The Red Circle Border represents *Karma* (energy). On the rank Certificate, the Kanji represents Universal Warrior Arts. For further information refer to the U.W.A. testing booklet.

The Yin and Yang

The outer circle is black and the inner circle is white, with the entire circle being symbolic of two fish. If one were to pick any one point in the circle, they would find that point unbroken. This means there is complete harmony between the white fish and the black fish. In addition, the yin and the yang also symbolize one being in tune with the universe, nature, and one's spirit (one's self). That is the principle that all should strive for complete harmony with one's self.

The Dragon (Chinese)

The dragon is an age-old symbol of the highest spiritual essence embodying wisdom, strength and divine power to transform the spirit.

Universal Warrior's Motto

I am a "New Age" Universal Warrior. I will use my **Warrior Arts ®** knowledge and skills to defend my family, my honor, my country and my principles. I will not react out of anger. In fact, my attitude will reflect and represent that of a positive person of good moral character and a disciplined student of the Martial Arts World.

<u>September 11, 2001</u>

The Day the Terrorists Attacked America

By Grandmaster Austin Wright Sr.*

The Terrorists have finally struck America,

Our American People are in a state of hysteria.

People are worried and in a state of fear,

Because of the fact uncertainty and pandemonium is everywhere.

Our life that felt so safe and secure,

Has now been threatened, terrorized, and a chance of war…

We love America and we will stand strong,

To protect our freedom that we knew so long,

As an American I will stand by my oath,

To defend our Honor, God, Freedom, Principles, Country, and Family.

"Plan "before" an attack, "not after"

*For the prevention/intervention and "readiness" of a crisis or hostile situation(s). Think P.A.C.E. 911 (All Rights reserved, copyright 2002).

CHAPTER 4 - *Dedication*

The late Dr. James Lavender, at 78, was a pioneer in the chiropractic field and American Martial Arts.

This chapter is dedicated to Our American Judo-Jujutsu teacher, the late Dr. James Lavender. Hanshi Austin Wright received permission from his daughter, Amy Lavender, who is a student, to honor her father and have him remembered for his teachings and dedication to the Martial Arts World.

Dr. Lavender passed down his Kodokan (Judo/Jujutsu Way) knowledge and wisdom to Master Dennis Austin Wright Sr. at the age of 14, in the mid 1950's. Master Dennis Wright's formal training took place at the Bayonne Naval Academy, (AKA the Bayonne Military Ocean Terminal), for five years.

Grandmaster Austin Wright, Sr. gives homage to some of our American pioneers such as the late Dr. James Lavender for the Judo-Jujutsu Martial Arts skills that were passed down to Master Dennis A. Wright, Sr. and then to his son, Hanshi Austin Wright, Sr., who incorporated these skills into the U.W.A. System.

Dr. James Lavender was an Honorary 10th Degree Black Belt (Ju-Dan) in Combative Arts. He served with Special Troops, First Marine Division, Pioneers and Engineers during World War II, participating in the battles of Guadalcanal and the Solomon Islands. He was one of Bayonne's "greats" at the Bayonne Naval Academy. He supported Austin Wright's efforts and new system.

Personal Dedication to Dr. Lavender from
Grandmaster Austin Wright Sr.

"Leaders must get used to personal sacrifices, criticism, and rejection. Before one becomes accepted one must first be rejected, so as to become better prepared to prove one's theory. If the source of your thoughts are true, then you will receive all you need to achieve your goal or destination. Once you know your "purpose," you shall be a determined and seeking student…"

(Left to right) Grandmaster Austin Wright, Sr., Dr. James Lavender, and Hanshi Dennis Wright, Sr.

(Top Photo) Dennis Wright as a beginner, training with Dr. James Lavender in the late 1950's and early 1960's. (2nd and 3rd Photos) Dr. Lavender performing a Judo Throw

Grandmaster Dennis Wright, Sr. (seated front row) in the mid 1970's in his Sunday private class at the local traditional Isshin-Ryu Karate School in Bayonne, NJ.

Grandmaster Austin Wright, Sr. (front row -1st from left) in karate class with his brothers in the early 1970's. Dennis Wright, Jr. (back row - 2nd from left), David Wright (back row - 5th from left), and Danny Wright (front row - 5th from left)

(Left) Grandmaster *Austin Wright, Sr. performing an exhibition of a side kick at Sheppard AFB, TX.*
(Below Left) Grandmaster *Austin Wright, Sr. in the U.S. Air Force.*

Advertisements for the Wright's Dojo of Self-Defense featuring Hanshi Dennis A. Wright, Sr. (left ad) and Austin Wright, Jr. (right ad), the father and son, respectively of Grandmaster Austin Wright, Sr.

Hanshi Dennis Wright, Sr. (back row center) with members of Wright's Dojo of Self-Defense Saturday Karate Class.

Grandmaster Austin Wright, Sr. pictured with family at the 1991 "30+ Years in Martial Arts" Dinner held at the Bayonne Soccer Club. (Left to right) Hanshi Austin Wright, Sr., Mary Wright (Austin's Mother), Shihan Dennis Wright, Sr. (Austin's father), David Wright, Danny Wright, and Dwayne Wright (Austin's Brothers).

All six Wright Brothers and Father, Hanshi Dennis Wright, Sr. posing for a picture inside the Dojo of Self-Defense. From left to right: Dennis Wright, Jr., Danny Wright, Christopher Wright, Austin Wright, Sr., Dwayne Wright, and David Wright.

Grandmaster Austin Wright, Sr. seated in his office at the headquarters of the U.W.A. Federation of America, Inc. located at 16-18 West 9ʰ St. Bayonne, NJ.

Some of the Universal Warrior Arts Chief Instructors inside the Dojo. From left to right: (front row) Mr. Vito Doria, Mr. Mike Ostrowski, Mr. Antonio Wilson, Mr. Austin Wright, Jr., and Mr. Chester Kaminski. (Back row) Mr. Carmen Filippone, Mr. Jay Johnson, and Mr. Wayne Shivers. (Top center) Founder and President, Grandmaster Austin Wright, Sr.

(Top photo) Grandmaster Austin Wright, Sr. posing with nephew, Christopher Wright, Jr. (Middle photo) Austin Wright, Jr. holding his Grand Championship Karate trophy. (Bottom photo) Priscilla Y. Wright holding her "Outstanding Competitor for Sparring" trophy and Overall winner in the Juniors Division (Boys & Girls ages 10-12) trophy. Both Austin Jr. and Priscilla are third generation martial artists in the Wright's Family Lineage.

Action:
Lion Claw technique with Grandmaster Wright.

Dwayne Wright, U.W.A.'s TKO Cardio Kick-Boxing Instructor, New England Diamond Gloves Champion and Golden Gloves Champion.

The "Wright" Family Legacy

(Left to right) Grandmaster Austin Wright, Sr. and Hanshi Dennis Wright, Sr. shake hands during their partnership in the Wright's Dojo of Self-Defense (1990 - 1996).

CHAPTER 5 - Testimonials

From the Author

I, Grandmaster Austin Wright, Sr., testify that I am the author, creator, and founder of the Wright's Repertoire <u>U.W.A. System, Universal Dojo of Self-Defense, Inc, of Bayonne, N. J.</u> I am the Head Teacher of the Bayonne D.E.P. Self-Defense Program, Jersey City Karate League, Society Hill I Karate Club and the President of the U.W.A. Federation of America. I testify and certify that I am an American Veteran and former U.S. Air Force Instructor/Sargent, Karate Champion, and "New Age Warrior." I have been given the rights and blessings publicly from my teacher and father Master Dennis Austin Wright Sr. to go forth to sanction and promote the "Wright Family Legacy" which shall be known as **The Universal Warrior Arts System**. Then from this day forth, I testify that I will carry the torch that was passed onto me. I am no longer under my teacher's discipleship or jurisdiction. I publicly stated, "We the board members of the U.W.A. System and Students have nullified all our associations with our former local Karate Associations, due to our irreconcilable differences. We are advocates of a new radical restoration for "New Age Warriors," who are liberal, disciplined, serious, dedicated, and loyal to the Martial Arts world. We recognize those who put the efforts, energies, and time into their choice of "Art" or "Style."

In all there were three decades of formal and traditional training, as well as, street survival self-defense training passed down from Asian World Martial Arts to American Martial Arts History. This includes American Okinawan Isshin-Ryu Karate, American Judo/Jujutsu Combative Arts, American Kickboxing, and Chinese Tai Chi Chuan (Wu-Shu).

All of this has evolved and prepared me for my destiny. I am the Founder and Highest Ranking Authority of the U.W.A. System. I am

"American made," as was my teacher. I am the recipient of the "Life Time Achievement Award" for three decades of Martial Arts Training and have been recognized by various national organizations and promoters for my dedication and consistency to the national competition. In 2001, I was honored by the U.W.A Federation of America for becoming a three time National Champions Coach/Trainer (1999, 2000, & 2001).

In the book, "The Art of War" by Sun Tzu it states, *"Those who are skilled in combat do not become angered, and those who are skilled at winning do not become afraid. Thus the wise win before they fight, while the ignorant fight to win."*

I testify that the Universal Warrior Arts System is and will be my path and "way" of life. My entire life, destiny if you will, has prepared me for this leadership position today. For those who know me can and will attest to this. As for those who are my "emulators," "player haters," and "economic rivals," it really doesn't matter what they say or try to do, because resistance to the truth is futile. I shall train and teach my children and students the foundation and principles of the U.W.A. System concepts which were taught and passed down to me by my father/teacher, Dennis A, Wright, Sr. and evolved and patterned by the Universal Dojo of Self-Defense Inc., Board Members and myself.

In closing, I would like to state that there is a "time" for Action and Reaction, War and Peace, Worldly Times and Heavenly Times…"

Respectively yours,

Grandmaster Austin Wright, Sr., Founder

Testimonials of U.W.A. Chief Instructors

I, Sensei (Teacher) Michael Ostrowski, testify that I am a chief Instructor under the U.W.A. System. I am in good standings with Master Austin Wright, Sr. I am a Board Member of the U.W.A. Federation of America. I have been training for 18 years. I have trained in the Isshin-Ryu System in Bayonne, New Jersey. I started in that school as a child. Master Wright was also one of my instructors at that school, as well as his father, Master Dennis A. Wright Sr. I have achieved the rank of San Dan (3rd degree Black Belt) from my former Dojo, in Bayonne, NJ. Eventually, the Main "Dojo" was closed. Prior to the "Dojo's" closing, I was given notice and I left to continue training with Master A. Wright. Master Wright then re-trained me, motivated me, opened my mind, and promoted me to the rank of Yo-Dan (4th Degree Black Belt) in Isshin-Ryu Karate and Sho-Dan Black Belt in U.W.A. System, after several years.

Master Wright gave me permission to create a sword Kata under the U.W.A. System, called "Universal Sword I." I have my sword training from Aikido. I trained in Aikido for three years. I competed in a National Tournament under the U.W.A. Federation. I placed third in that tournament. I am presently still training and teaching at the Main Headquarters at Wright's Dojo.

Sincerely,

Michael Ostrowski, 6th Dan Chief Instructor and Board Member of the **U.W.A. Federation of America** Registration #0001; Student No. #0006

I, Sensei (Teacher) Mr. Carmen Filippone, testify that I am a U.W.A. Teacher in good standing. I am loyal to the promoting of the Art of the U.W.A. System and its cause. I am a certified Black Belt Instructor and Board Member. I am one of the chief Instructors at the Main Headquarters in Bayonne (V.F.W. #226 Post) and Chief Instructor at the Society Hill Clubhouse (Rt. 440, Jersey City, NJ). I have been training under the Wrights for eight years, and have a certified Isshin-Ryu Black Belt under Hanshi Dennis A. Wright Sr., and his son (registration #1233, O.I.K.A.) I also have a 3rd Dan in the U.W.A. System. I have developed two Jo Weapon Katas, known as Universal Jo I and Universal Jo II. I am honored to train under Hanshi Austin Wright Sr., because he teaches "sport" and "practical" Martial Arts, head instructor of the Italy International, U.W.A. branch.

Sincerely,

Sensei Carmen Filippone, 5th Dan and Chief Instructor of the **U.W.A. Federation of America** Registration #0003; Student No. #0008

■■■

It was Bruce Lee that captured my attention. Like so many other youngsters at that time, he was as prolific as the Green Hornet that I just had to know how to kick that fast and punch that hard. I joined the Eagle Claw Kung Fu Academy in 1964, where I trained for four years.

It was the dawn of the Age of Aquarius, one of the best slogans I ever heard at that time. I joined the army to see the world. So on November 22, 1967, I did. Leaving from Fort Hamilton to Fort Jackson, South Carolina, my journey began from Fort Jackson to Fort Brag Jump School, to Fort Belvoir, Virginia Engineer School. This is where I learned that my older brother was drafted to go to Vietnam. So, I volunteered at age 19, what I knew about anything. I thought I was still going to see the world. We left for Vietnam from Seattle to Honolulu, Hawaii, then to Wake Island, from Wake Island to Camron Bay, Vietnam.

When we got off the plane, the climate was the first thing that told us that we were not in Kansas anymore. It was literally 110 degrees at night. That same night we experienced our first taste of combat. While waiting to be processed, at 19, in a foreign land, 12:00 midnight, no weapon, bombs going off around you, and you don't know where to go for cover. Then finding a spot that you think is safe and still could not escape the mosquitoes, the size of a B52 airplane, and the scorching weather. The following morning, after the excitement, we were greeted by what became the new slogan "GOOOOD Morning Vietnam."

We were gathered in one large group that morning after breakfast in a muddy field. There was an NCO standing on a 55 gallon drum of diesel fuel (I found out later that it was not only for the trucks, but it was also used as fuel for burning fecal matter). He stretched his hand out, as if he was parting the waters like Moses. He said, "Those on the right go south, those on the left go north." As for my training as a generator operator, that soon became a thing of the past. I was now a foot soldier (more commonly known as a grunt). That was when I really began to see the world and its splendor.

Sometimes it was a walk in the sun, the beautiful rolling mountains, the lush rice patties and their amazing irrigation systems, an ancient temple-a virtual Sunday drive. No one called it that until the unit was back at the base camp, because at that point any number of bad things could happen. At every step there were the myriad dangers of Vietnam: ambush, booby traps, land mines, snipers, leeches, and those B52 mosquitoes. Traveling through the country you see the beauty of the land and the bitterness of war. After my time was up in Vietnam, I came back home through California, where we met with hostility from the anti-war demonstrators. It left a very bitter taste in my mouth. It made me question patriotism. What was it all about? I returned to Eagle Claw Kung Fu to resume my training. After a while, working and training became a struggle in itself. With a growing family, training, and working, it became very difficult. Trying to steal one hour of training time, having no time for lunch, my training became more of street/combat training. We were applying techniques that I was taught by a Korean Martial Artist, while in Vietnam.

I moved to Bayonne. When my daughter expressed interest in a Karate School down the block. I brought her down just to take a look. That is all it took to rekindle that old flame in me. The dojo was the Wright's Dojo of Self-Defense. When my daughter and I entered, we were greeted warmly. I watched the class. The instructor, who clearly knew what he was doing, impressed me. He was firm and sometimes jovial. What impressed me the most was that he took time to answer questions from kids that had problems with the lesson? Before leaving, my daughter became a member of the Dojo of Self-Defense. After attending two more kid classes, I stayed to observe the instructor with the adults in the class. It was a no nonsense class. I thought he was trying to impress me, but after joining and training with this instructor, who I chose to call Shihan Austin Wright Sr., I found out that he was not trying to impress me, but wanted to show me that it's like that all the time. No nonsense since that first day.

Since I started training with Shihan Austin Wright Sr. I have won several Inter-Dojo Grand Championships. In 1999 and 2000, I won the National Championships in Atlantic City, New Jersey. I am now a Board Member of the Universal Dojo of Self-Defense, and a Senior Chief Instructor. I was also given the right by Shihan Austin Wright Sr., to create my own Sai Kata which is known as Antonio Sai I. Austin Wright Sr. is not only my Shihan, but also one of my best friends. I know that patriotism comes in many shapes, forms, and styles. I can now say that I have found patriotism in the men and women of the Universal Dojo of Self-Defense.

Sincerely,

Antonio Wilson, 5th. Dan Chief Instructor and Board Member of the **U.W.A. Federation of America** Registration #0004; Student No. #0010

I, Chester Kaminski, Ni-Dan in Isshin-Ryu Karate, have been affiliated with the Wright Family Karate Program since February 1992. My original instructor was Mr. Dennis A. Wright, Sr., 8th Dan in the Isshin-Ryu style. He taught me the basics, katas, and helped me develop fighting techniques. Several years later, his son, Austin Wright, Sr., developed an eclectic style that seemed to suit me better.

Together we have built a friendship, and he has helped me to understand the concepts of the Universal Warrior Arts. These concepts have allowed us to open up programs throughout Hudson County. We currently are teaching at Society Hill in Jersey City, P.S. # 11 in Jersey City, and the Veterans of Foreign Wars HQ #226 in Bayonne.

As a chief instructor to Austin Wright, Sr., it has been my honor to witness the development of a truly unique style. This style has brought him consecutive National titles in 1999, 2000, 2001 and 2002. It has also given everyone affiliated with this style a sense of accomplishment.

No one knows what the future holds, but we all hope that this new adventure continues and opens up a panorama of knowledge to everyone that seeks it.

Sincerely,

Chester Kaminski, 5th. Dan Chief Instructor and Board Member of the **U.W.A. Federation of America** Registration #0002; Student #0009

■■

I consider it an honor and privilege to write this testimonial for Grandmaster Austin Wright, Sr. Grandmaster Wright has been a tremendous source of inspiration and motivation for me, and over the years, guided me to embrace a better balance of mind, body and spirit.

I consider Grandmaster Wright to be an exemplary role model with impeccable character and unyielding integrity. No matter the adversity or life challenges Grandmaster Wright encounters, he has an uncanny ability to remain calm, in control, positive and optimistic, and serve as a source of strength for others.

Grandmaster Wright has dedicated his life to the advancement of the Martial Arts. The depth of his knowledge and ability to apply the principles to everyday life scenarios separates him from others. Grandmaster Wright emphasizes that the concepts and skills learned in the Dojo are equally applicable to real world scenarios, focusing on battlefield readiness, preparation, and training. As a practicing attorney, I oftentimes engage my inner Warrior to advance the cause of my clients, mindful that the goal is Peace before War.

Although Grandmaster Wright is an awe-inspiring force as a Martial Artist, he has a gentle spirit, is open, very kind, considerate, and always thoughtful of others. Grandmaster Wright remains indiscriminately available and willing to help anyone in need, and encourages his students and instructors to follow his lead.

Grandmaster Wright works very hard. He has a full time job, and manages to mentor his students both inside and outside the Dojo, spend quality time with his family, and attend weekly religious services.

Above all, I consider Grandmaster Wright a trusted and genuine friend. Since my work schedule limits my ability to train in the Dojo, Grandmaster Wright trains with me very early in the morning before work and on weekends. His selfless and steadfast ideologies empower me to be a better Martial Artist, husband, father, coach, friend, attorney, etc., by nurturing my Fighting Spirit.

Sincerely,

Anthony Bianciella Esq.

(Left to Right) Grand Master Austin Wright Sr. and Dr. James Thomas awarding Master Wright with an International World Grand Championship Belt in Trelawney, Jamaica 2005 www.usnmat.net

Closing Message from
the President & the Founder

In closing, I would like to say Now is the time for Action! By an effort of will, change of attitude, and spirituality, we shall overcome most of our challenges. We as members of one another, must defend our Liberty, minds, and basic human rights through awareness, discipline and defense. Our ancestors and pioneers fought that fight of oppression, cruelty, and anarchy not too long ago. Self-Defense is like basic training of the mind, body, spirit and intellect. Knowledge of Martial Arts science, principles, peace tactics and Battlefield Readiness 101 should be "taught to all."

ACKNOWLEDGEMENTS

First, I would like to give thanks, praise, and acknowledgement to the Infinite Almighty God, and Highest Power. I have been humbled and evolved by Life and Nature's experiences/lessons many times. I have found peace of mind and enrichment of spirit while fasting, praying, meditating, and reading spiritual Universal books of knowledge from different parts of the world such as America, Asia, India, South America, Africa, and Europe. All have their history and truth based upon their perception, point of view, and experiences.

Yet, I have been reminded throughout my life of Bible verses that are from my child/adulthood, and are a part of my thinking and my heritage. The embedded ones are: John 3:16, Psalms 23, Ephesians 4:17, in particular Zechariah 4:6 "Not by Might nor by Power, but by My Spirit, says the Lord of Hosts." And finally the Serenity Prayer.

I give thanks to my Mother (Mary U. Kelly-Wright) and Father (Dennis A. Wright, Sr.), who always did their best. Love, peace and happiness always. I would like to thank my father, Dennis Austin Wright, Sr., for allowing me to fly, and promote our Wright Family Legacy.

Next, I would like to give thanks to my family members, friends, and mentors, who inspired me and believed in me: Estela M. Ramos, Nelfa M. Wright and Jocelyn Brea, Alicia Kelly Smith (My godmother), all the family members of the late Thomas L. Wright, Sr., Paul E. Wright, Sr. and Reverend Elmer C. Wright, the late Lola Delaney, the late Barbara Townes, the late Marjorie Wright, the late Gertrude Porch, Simon Kelly (Fellow Army Veteran), uncle Jude Kelly, my Aunt Frances Baker Wright, my cousin Mark A. (Wright) Muhammad, John & Rita Wondolowski, Mr. Michael Hurley Sr., Mr. James (Jimmie) Jackson, Brian Rowan, Antoine Allen, Mrs. Charlene Edwards, Glenn Porch and the entire Porch family, my brothers

(Dennis, Jr., David, Daniel, Dwayne, and Chris Wright), and the entire Kelly and Wright Families.

Thanks to all of my mentors, instructors, and students: my Pop Warner Football Coach and longtime friend Joe Di Giorio, Amy Lavender and Mrs. Lavender, Mr. Mike Ostrowski, Mr. Carmen Filippone, Mr. Antonio Wilson, Mr. Mark Sommers, Mr. Chester Kaminski, Dr. Dennis P. McCarthy, Anthony Bianciella Esq. and all students of martial arts and U.W.A. Black Belts.

A special thanks and appreciation goes to my son, Austin Joél Wright, Jr., third generation martial artist, grand champion and world champion, also to my daughter, Priscilla Yansey Wright, third generation Black Belt, 3rd Dan and loyal daughter.

Throughout one's life, you have many teachers, nurturers, and guides. I would like to acknowledge them as follows: my Mother, Mary Wright, Antonio Wilson (Advisor/Friend), Francis Baker Wright (Aunt), Mark A. (Wright) Muhammad (Cousin), John and Sandy Smith, James Clemento, Rose Santiago, uncle Jude Kelly, Miguel (Mike) Diaz, and family Friends and childhood guides.

To Josie and Bob Cleary, my right-hand administrative helpers and beloved and dear friends. To Marisol Cerdeira and Carmela Pallotta who helped us edit this book. To my beloved and dear friends and motivators Barbara Weir, Nicky D'Anna, and Ronald Townes Sr. Bruce Dillin (of Dillin Tires), Vito Doria, Sr. (Bayonne Soccer Club), Tony Gonzalez, Kevin Rankin, Tony Mazza, and the late Bob Crute (of Hi-Tech Cleaners).

U.W.A. Federation of America Ranking System

* *

1st	Belt	Level I	White Belt	10th Kyu
2nd	Belt		White Belt- 1 Stripe	9th Kyu
3rd	Belt		White Belt- 2 Stripes	8th Kyu
4th	Belt		Yellow Belt	7th Kyu
5th	Belt		Blue Belt	6th Kyu
6th	Belt	Level II	Green Belt	5th Kyu
7th	Belt		Green Belt-1 Stripe	4th Kyu
8th	Belt	Level III	Brown Belt	3rd Kyu
9th	Belt		Brown Belt 1 stripe	2nd Kyu
10th	Belt		Brown Belt 2 stripes	1st Kyu

* *

Sho Dan	Level IV	Black Belt	1st Degree
Ni Dan		Black Belt	2nd Degree
San Dan		Black Belt	3rd Degree
Yo Dan		Black/Red Stripes	4th Degree
Go Dan	Level V	Black/Red Tips	5th Degree

* *

Roku Dan	Level VI	Red & Black Belt	6th Degree
Shichi Dan	Level VII	Red & Black Belt	7th Degree
Hachi Dan	Level VIII	Red & Black Belt	8th Degree
Ku Dan	Level IX	Red Belt	9th Degree
Ju Dan	Level X	Red Belt	10th Degree

* *

1st & 2nd Dan- Sempei (Certified Instructor)

3rd Dan - Sensei (Teacher)

4th Dan- Renshi (Chief and Head Teacher)

5th, 6th & 7th - (Master)

8th - Master Teacher

9th- Grand Master

10th Dan - Soke (Grand Master - Head of Family – Founder)

Brown Belt - Assistant Instructor

Junior Brown Belt – Junior Helper & Assistant

Junior Black Belt – Black & White Belt (Jr. Warriors)

U.W.A. Instructor Lineage - Chief Instructors (CI)*

Austin Wright, Sr. (Soke) - 10th Dan, Founder, President & Director of U.W. A.

(CI)Austin Wright, Jr. (Bloodline) – 5th Dan Black Belt Chief Instructor*

(CI)Priscilla Wright (Bloodline) – 3rd Dan Black Belt

(CI)Mr. Mike Ostrowski - 6th Dan Chief Instructor

(CI)Mr. Antonio Wilson – 6th Dan, Chief Instructor

(CI)Mr. Chester Kaminski - 6th Dan, Chief Instructor*, Jersey City, NJ Branch

(CI)Mr. Carmen Filippone - 5th Dan, Chief Instructor*, International Italy Branch

Mr. Vito Doria, Jr. – 5th Dan

Mr. Wayne Shivers - 5th Dan

Mr. Joseph McNamara- 4th Dan

Mr. Timmy Prisk – 4th Dan (Yo-Dan) Isshin-Ryu

Mr. William Vaughn – 3rd Dan Irvington, NJ Branch

Kenneth Jackson – 3rd Dan

(CI)Mr. Kenneth Thompson- 2nd Dan

Mr. Christopher Simpson- 2nd Dan

Mr. Chris Shaw Sr., - 1st Dan

Mr. John O'Brien - 1st Dan

(CI)Mr. Donald Keith Price – 1st Dan

Procedure for Tying the Belt (Obi)

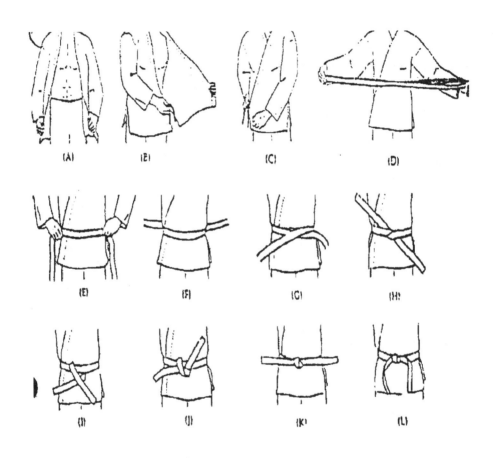

U.W.A. Federation - *Test of Knowledge*
WHITE BELT 10th *Kyu*

White Belts are obligated to learn basic terminology, rules & procedures of the dojo. Each student of Karate, Jujutsu, & Kickboxing (Karate-Ka) is mandated to perform basic introductory moves before progressing to a higher rank. This progression is determined by the <u>Sensei</u> <u>or</u> <u>Head Teacher</u> in charge.

1. <u>Know all the Rules and Procedures.</u>

2. <u>When do we bow?</u>

    Enter/Exit/To each other

3. <u>Why do we bow?</u>

    For courtesy & respect

4. <u>When do we line up?</u>

    In the beginning and end of class, and when the class is called to attention (ex: when Shihan enters the Dojo or when he or a substitute teacher is lecturing)

5. <u>How do we line up?</u>

    By rank order (lowest to highest belt color)

6. <u>How do we address our Instructors in class?</u>

    Mr._____Sensei_____Shihan.

7. <u>Learn Stances:</u>

   1. Attention Stance (Dachi)

   2. Toe to Heel Stance

   3. Pyramid Stance

8. <u>Know how to step forward and backwards with balance.</u>

   5 Basics (Upper body exercise)

   2 Kicks

9. <u>Know the following in Japanese:</u>

   Yame-   **Stop**

   Kiot Skay-   **Attention**

   Rei-   **Bow**

   Surate-   **Sit**

   Kata-   **Form**

White Belt - 1 Stripe 9th Kyu (First Rank Testing)

1. <u>Name the founder (Soke) of the U.W.A. System.</u>

   Grand Master Austin Wright Sr.

The Patches of the U.W.A.

New Universal Warrior Arts System:

I. Black Background **Represents: The Universe/Infinity**

II. Red Circle Exterior Border **Represents: Energy (Karma)**

III. Yin-Yang **Represents: Balance, the outer circle is black, the inner circle is white. The entire circle is symbolic of two fish. In addition, the Yin and the Yang also symbolize one being in tune with the universe, nature, and one's spirit (one's self). That is the principle that all should strive for - complete harmony with one's self. (For example: Man/Woman, Hard/Soft, Hot/Cold, Peace/War, Love/Hate, and degrees of the two. In conclusion, all things have opposites, yet are complimentary to each other.**

IV. Right Closed Fist: **War**

V. Left Open Hand: **Peace**

FIVE ELEMENTS OF THE U.W.A. PATCH

Japanese Writing on Patch:

VI. Bottom: **(Earth) – Habitation, Body, and Nature**

VII. Left Side: **(Wind) - Air in Motion: Movement, Speed, and Vibration**

VIII.   Top: **(Fire) - Self-Control: Emotions, Intellect, and Ki (Inner Spirit)**

IX. Right Side: **(Water) – Liquid, Meditation, and Fluid Motion**

X. Iron: **Symbolic to the patch itself. Ironbound, Unyielding, Action & Reaction, intensity, discipline, defense, and an honest self-expression of one's self. "ALL is MIND" (The Kybalion)**

THE U.W.A. MEMBERSHIP PATCH

The dragon is an age-old symbol of the highest spiritual essence embodying wisdom and power to transform the spirit.

1. Name the Origin of the various styles of Martial Arts.

   China, Okinawa, Japan, and the U.S.A.

2. Know 5 Basics, 3 Kicks, and 1 Law

3. Know Universal Law #1

   Train your body, mind, and spirit in balance and harmony.

4. Know the following in Japanese:

   Belt - Obi

   Karate Uniform - GI

   Sit - Aswatti

5. Count from 1 to 10 in Japanese

   Ichi, Ni, San, Shi, Go, Roku, Shichi, Hachi, Ku, and Ju.

6. Know the procedure for tying the Belt (Obi)

White Belt - Two Stripes 8th Kyu

1. <u>What is the meaning of Universal?</u>

    For all.

2. <u>What is the meaning of Warrior?</u>

    One who is experienced in U.W.A. concepts/training?

3. <u>What is the meaning of Arts?</u>

    A craft or the creation of beautiful things.

4. <u>Know 10 Basics and 6 Kicks</u>

5. <u>Know the following in Japanese:</u>

Acknowledgement-	**Osu!**
Line Up–	**Yame!**
Karate-	**Empty hand**
Begin-	**Hai Jimme!**
Martial Arts Gym-	**Dojo**
Free style match–	**Kumite**

6. <u>Know Universal Laws of Training.</u>

    Know #1 & #2

    #2 deals with fears

<u>Yellow Belt 7th Kyu</u>

Universal Taikeoku (Basic Form of Blocks, Strikes, & Balance)

1. <u>Name the system of our style of martial arts and where it originated.</u>
   Universal Warrior Arts, Bayonne, N. J., U.S.A.

2. <u>Name the founder of the Universal Warrior Arts System.</u>
   Hanshi Austin Wright Sr.

3. <u>Meaning of Universal.</u>
   For all

4. <u>Why do we bow?</u>
   Courtesy & Respect

5. <u>When do we bow?</u>
   Enter/Exit/To each other

6. <u>What does the word *karate* mean?</u>
   Empty Hand

7. <u>How do you address your instructor (3rd Dan or higher) in class?</u>
   Sensei

8. <u>Count from 1 to 10 in Japanese.</u>
   Ichi, Ni, San, Shi, Go, Roku, Shichi, Hachi, Ku, Ju

9. <u>Why did Hanshi Austin Wright Sr. develop the Universal Warrior Arts system?</u>

So that one can learn a variety of eclectic martial arts in One style.

10. <u>Know the following in Japanese:</u>

Stop-   **Yame**

Attention-   **Kiot Skay**

Bow-   **Rei**

Sit-   **Surwatti**

Karate Uniform-   **Gi**

REVIEW   REVIEW   REVIEW

<u>KNOW TAIKEOKU BUNKAI (explanation of moves)</u>

Blue Belt 6th Kyu

1. <u>What is the meaning of Martial Arts?</u>

    It is a version of the original warrior way concept.

2. <u>Why did Hanshi Austin Wright Sr. develop the Universal Warrior Arts System?</u>

    He developed it so that one can learn a variety of traditional and practical martial arts in one style.

3. <u>What are some titles of the Highest Instructors called?</u>

    Shihan, Master Instructor, Soke, and Grand Master (Hanshi).

    3.A. <u>Count from 1 - 15 in Japanese</u>

    **Ichi, Ni, San, Shi, Go, Roku, Shichi, Hachi, Ku, Ju,
    Ju-Ichi, Ju- Ni, Ju-San, Ju-Shi, Ju-Go.**

4. <u>Perform 10 Kicks</u>

5. <u>Know 5 Universal Laws of Training.</u>

REVIEW   REVIEW   REVIEW
KNOW TAIKYOKU and EARTH KATA BUNKAI

Green Belt 5th & 4th Kyu

1. <u>Name the three basic stances:</u>

    Pyramid Stance, Horse Stance, Cat Stance

2. <u>Name three Japanese techniques:</u>

Tsuki Waza	**Punching Techniques**
Nage Waza	**Throwing Techniques**
Geri Waza	**Kicking Techniques**

3. <u>Name several hand techniques:</u>

Shuto = Chop	**Cork Screw Punch**
Nukite = Spear thrust	**Spinning Back Hand**
Uraken = Back Fist	**Spinning Shuto**
Tutsui = Hammer Fist	

4. <u>Name all the kyu belt ranks:</u>

White Belt	**10^t Kyu**	**Green Belt**	**4th Kyu**
White Belt (1)	**9th Kyu**	**Brown Belt**	**3rd Kyu**
White Belt (2)	**8th Kyu**	**Brown Belt**	**2nd Kyu**
Yellow Belt	**7th Kyu**	**Brown Belt**	**1st Kyu**
Blue Belt	**6th Kyu**		
Green Belt	**5th Kyu**		

5. <u>Name the Katas required for promotion to Brown Belt.</u>

    Taikeoku, Earth, Wind & Fire.

6. <u>Count from 1 to 20 in Japanese:</u>

Ichi, Ni, San, Shi, Go, Roku, Shichi, Hachi, Ku, Ju,Ju-Ichi, Ju-Ni, Ju-San, Ju-Shi, Ju-Go, Ju-Roku, Ju-Shichi, Ju-Hachi, Ju-Ku, Ni-Ju

7. <u>Explain the Triad Theory of Mind, Body, and Spirit in your own Words.</u>

8. <u>Know the following rank terminology in Japanese:</u>

       Student (Brown Belt & below) – Kyu

       Instructor – Sempei (1st & 2nd Dan)

       Teacher – Sensei (3rd Dan & up)

       Dan - Black Belt and Above

       Grand Master (9th to 10th Dan)

       Founder – Soke (Highest Rank)

Name someone who brought about radical revolutionary change in the martial arts from Hong Kong to America.

9. <u>What are some of the combined styles of the Universal Warrior Arts System?</u>

   Judo, Jujutsu, Okinawan Karate, Kung Fu, and American Kick-Boxing.

10. <u>Know vital points, Ju-Jutsu/Judo principals, and develop self-Control.</u>

11. <u>What is the translation of Universal Warrior Arts?</u>

   "The All Changing Warrior"

Brown Belt 3ʳᵈ Kyu

All requirements of 7ᵗʰ Kyu through 3ʳᵈ Kyu plus:

1. Name three kicking techniques.

   Mae- Keage Geri   **Front Kick**

   Mae-Washi Geri   **Roundhouse Kick**

   Ushiro Geri   **Back Kick**

2. Know the following in Japanese:

   Earth = Chi

   Wind = Baram

   Fire = Bool

   Water = Mul

3. Know Universal Warrior Arts in Japanese.

   Universal = Chunsae Kae

   Warrior = Mu

   Arts = Sool

2. Know the following in Japanese:

   Earth = Chi

   Wind = Baram

   Fire = Bool

   Water = Mul

3. Know Universal Warrior Arts in Japanese.

   Universal = Chunsae Kae

   Warrior = Mu

   Arts = Sool

Brown Belt 2nd Kyu

All requirements of 9th Kyu through 3rd Kyu plus:

1. Say the following in Japanese:

Referee-	**Sinbon**
Karate Student-	**Karate-Ka**
One Full Point-	**Ippon**
Focus-	**Kime**

2. Count from 1 to 30 in Japanese:

Ichi, Ni, San, Shi, Go, Roku, Shichi, Hachi, Ku, Ju,

Ju-Ichi, Ju-Ni, Ju-San, Ju-Shi, Ju-Go, Ju-Roku,

Ju-Shichi, Ju-Hachi, Ju-Ku, Ni-Ju, Ni-Ju-Ichi, Ni-Ju-Ni,

Ni-Ju-San, Ni-Ju-Shi, Ni-Ju-Go, Ni-Ju-Roku,

Ni-Ju-Shichi, Ni-Ju-Hachi, Ni-Ju-Ku, San-Ju

Brown Belt 1st Kyu

(THE BELT OF ASCENSION)

Ascension - To give up, to rise.

All requirements of 9th Kyu through 2nd Kyu plus:

Know entire vocabulary & terminology, Jujutsu/Judo principles and self-defense techniques

1. Name some of the weapons used in the U.W.A. System.

    *Bo

    *Jo

    *Sai

    *Nunchaku

2. Know the following in Japanese:

    Inner Strength - Ki

    Breaking- Tameshi-Wari

    Spirit or Way of the Warrior – Bushido

3. Name two martial arts systems:

    Jujutsu   Judo

4. Develop and expand your knowledge of U.W.A. principles in:

    A. **Katas**

    B. **Weapons**

    C. **Philosophy**

5.   Demonstration of skills and/or knowledge through class participation.

    A. Leading the class in exercises.

    B. Leading the class in basic stances, blocks, & punches.

    C. Leading the class in kicks.

    D. Leading the class in Practical Self-Defense.

6. Socialization Skills

    To take part in meetings. Form a Junior Black Belt and Brown Belt Club. Meetings should be held one or two times per month. You can discuss techniques and activities to support personal and social growth, in the format of the adult meetings. Discussion of etiquette, manners, and safety awareness should be the topics of meetings.

7. Develop One Personalized Kata and memorize it.

Black Belt Certification

1ST Dan

All requirements of 9th Kyu through 1st Kyu plus:

1. Perform five Element Katas and Know the Bunkai.

   Taikeoku (Master D. Wright's), Earth, Wind, Fire, Water, & Iron Forms.

2. Board Breaking

   Three board minimum

3. Endurance Tests

   Jog 1 ½ miles and other endurance tests (Kumite, Bag Training, Self-Defense, & Calisthenics).

4. Experience: 3 to 5 years (Adults) & 3 to 5 years (Kids) Junior Black Belt.

   Have a minimum of two years' experience instructing in a traditional/formal setting.

5. Perform continuous sparring or competition in the arena (Tournaments).

6. Know Practical Self-Defense

7. Always present a good attitude, discipline, and loyalty to Your teacher (Sensei) and Dojo.

8. Iron Kata shall be practiced "after" Black Belt Testing (Certification).

The Universal Warrior Arts Laws of Training:

1. Train your body, mind and spirit in balance and Harmony.

2. Deal with Fears (fear of being hurt, fear or speaking out, Fear of looking foolish, and fear of change).

3. Establish attainable goals in life.

4. Take risks!! Think positively, believe you can.

5. Practice outside the Dojo (Speed, Power, & Ki).

6. Avoid negative self-fulfilling prophecies.

7. Practice respect, love, peace, courtesy and most of all Judge not, think before you speak (Do not let your Emotions override your intellect). Treat other people like You would like to be treated.

8. Honor your parents and respect the law.

9. Reflect and meditate on positive and negative events.

10. Knowledge is power, and for each level of knowledge, You are held responsible for how you use it.

Codes of U.W.A. System

1. Practice meditation and visualization.

2. Knowing others is wisdom, knowing yourself is enlightenment (Zen)

3. Train with openness, integrity, a positive attitude and a growing spirit!

4. Always look to evolve and reach the next level of your training!

5. Control your impulsiveness!

6. Utilize all of your "senses' (5) to include your "gut instincts or feelings."

7. Be yourself and know thy self. "Compliment Others"

8. Remember a small fire can burn down the whole forest....

9. Tie two birds together, though they have four wings they cannot fly. Why? (Zen)

10. "Discipline" and "Defense," You can't have one without the other.

11. The way of the Monkey (bully) is to walk around him, unmask his ego and you will find a coward disguised as a Monkey. (Zen)

12. Get set! strategize, strike hard, strike fast, and be deceptive.

13. Break your opponent's illusions and you will unveil their weaknesses.

14. Do not react out of "anger" or "frustration"!

15. Redirect or Parry negative energy forces.

16. "Appreciate" constructive criticism.

17. Avoid being oppositional, argumentative, judging, defiant, disruptive, rude, disrespectful, reckless, and angry! This lowers stress, and promotes a good character.

18. Look for solutions to "conflicts" and resolutions to your problems. When in doubt, seek help out!

19. Practice the P.A.C.E. 911 drill.

20. Students should balance their mind, body, and spirit.

STANCES OF U.W.A. SYSTEM

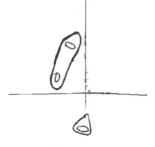

ANGLE AND LINEAR STANCES

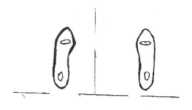

PYRAMID STANCE

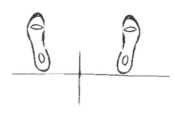

HORSE STANCE

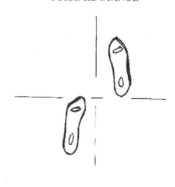

TOE TO HEEL STANCE

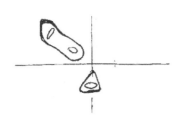

CRANE STANCE

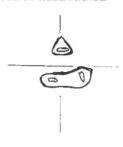

CAT STANCE

NOTE: Footwork and movements shall be practiced in "various" ways, not obvious patterns.... For instance, circular, crab-movements, criss-cross, bouncing, angles, linear, broken patterns and natural movements. One should counter strike, take down and subdue, etc. Stances should vary depending on scenarios and size of opponent(s).

UNIVERSAL STRIKNG CHART

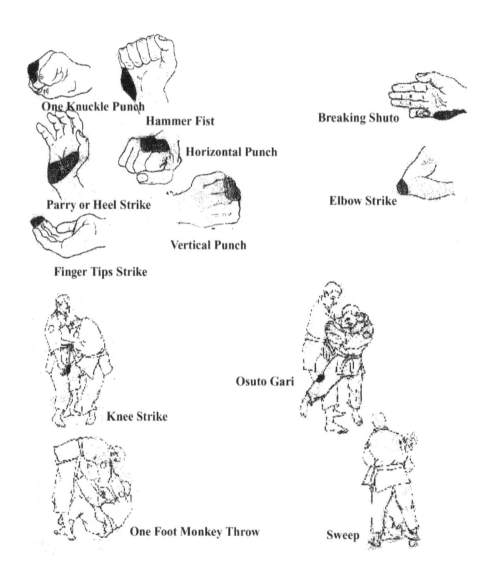

One Knuckle Punch

Hammer Fist

Breaking Shuto

Horizontal Punch

Parry or Heel Strike

Elbow Strike

Vertical Punch

Finger Tips Strike

Osuto Gari

Knee Strike

One Foot Monkey Throw

Sweep

Universal Striking Chart

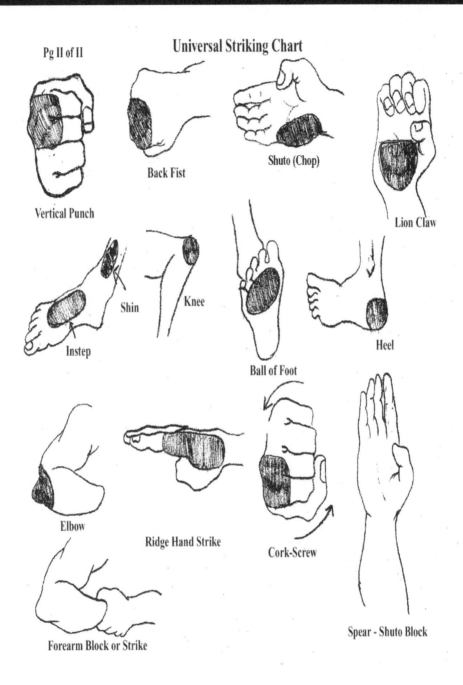

Vertical Punch

Back Fist

Shuto (Chop)

Lion Claw

Shin

Knee

Instep

Ball of Foot

Heel

Elbow

Ridge Hand Strike

Cork-Screw

Forearm Block or Strike

Spear - Shuto Block

Wright's U.W.A. Karate Team Wins World International Championship 2005

The Wright's Universal Warrior Art's Karate Team was successful in competing at the International World Championship "Freedom Games" which were held in Trelawney-Jamaica on June 2005 which is the 1st qualifier for the 2008 Olympics. After being scouted for 2 years by Dr. Jim Thomas – Head Coach of the U.S. National Martial Arts Team. Wright's U.W.A. karate school was extended an invitation to compete with other U.S. National Martial Arts Teams from the United States. The U.S. Martial Arts Team competed against other countries like Great Britain, Canada, and Jamaica just to name a few.

The Wright's U.W.A. National Karate Team went on short notice not knowing what to expect but prepared for action in Artistic Forms, Weapons, Freestyle Ju-Jutsu, and Point Sparring.

Below is a listing of our accomplishments at the Freedom Games.

<u>Masters Division:</u>

Grandmaster Austin Wright Sr. – Won a World International Point Grand Championship Belt for coming in 1st in Weapons, Kata and Point Sparring and an additional Belt for Best Dojo Support.

Senior Black Belt Division:

Wayne Shivers Black Belt 3rd Dan– 1st in Point Sparring, and 2nd in Kata

Vito Doria Black Belt 2nd Dan– 2nd in Point Sparring

Black Belt Division:

Michael Ostrowski Black Belt 5th Dan– 3rd in Point Sparring

Austin Wright Jr. Black Belt 3rd Dan –, 1st Point Fighting, 1st Ju-Jutsu, and 3rd Kata

Eulices Mateo Black Belt 1st Dan– 2nd in Point Sparring and **3rd** Continuous Fighting

Teen Women Black Belt / Brown Belt Division:

Priscilla Wright Black Belt 1st Dan– 1st in Kata, 1st in Point Sparring

Shanaya McNeil Brown Belt– 1st in Point Sparring and 2nd in Kata

Jr. Brown Belt Division:

Nick DeRos Brown Belt– 4th in Point Sparring and 4th in the Kiai Contest

Teens Green Belt Division:

Timothy Muise Green Belt– 2nd in Point Sparring and 3rd in Kata

Jr. Green Belt Division:

Giuseppe Ippolito Green Belt– 2nd Kata and 3rd in Point Sparring

Women's Blue Belt Division:

Deana Lubach Blue Belt– 1st in Kata and 1st Point Sparring

Women's Novice Division:

Jocelyn Brea White Belt– 1st in Point Sparring

Honorable Mentioned:

Kenneth Jackson Jr. Green Belt

Chester Kaminski Black Belt 4th Dan– Received an Outstanding Coach Award

In closing, we would like to thank Dr. Thomas (for the opportunity), our local business establishments and parents, friends, and Bayonne local residents who donated their time and money to help us fulfill our mission to attend the "Freedom Games". We will be attending the next Qualifier, which may be held in Ireland in June 2006

All students' train under direct supervision of Head Coach Grandmaster Austin Wright Sr. and certified Coaches and Instructors at the main Universal Warrior Martial Arts Headquarters located in Bayonne, New Jersey.

International "Alliance" Recognizes Austin Wright as 10th Degree Black Belt 2007

Austin Wright has become one of the most famous names upcoming in the Martial Arts World recognized as a Top Rated Coach, Author and 2005 World Karate Champion. He is an "Outstanding Instructional Leader" Writes Grandmaster Y.K. Kim of Martial Arts World Magazine competing 2007. Also, an "International Leader" Writes Grandmaster James Thomas USA Hall of Fame Head Coach. Wright's leadership skills in and out of the competition arena helped the U.S Team become a "Dominating Force" at the 2005 "Freedom Games" Jamaica. He won (3) Gold medals and (1) Grand Belt to assist the U.S Team. Also, Wright had brought one of the largest winning teams from N.J.

The 2007 USA Hall of Fame Inductee Banquet was held in New York at the Sheraton Marriot where Austin Wright was awarded an Official Black Belt Rank Certificate for the Grade of 10th Degree Black Belt by an International Ranking Advisor Board of Directors; Hirouki Matumoto 10thDan from Japan, Jesus Rodriguez 10thDan from Mexico, M.J. Tianero 10th Dan from Saudi Arabia, James Rosenbauch 10th Dan from Nebraska USA and Dr. Jim Thomas 10th Dan from Ohio USA just to name a few.

Dr. Thomas states "Wright's credentials are Top Rated." He has been established since 1985 and was also a Former U.S. Air Force Instructor.

Mr. Wright has been appointed a second term as the N.J. State Director for the US National Martial Arts Team "Alliance" for 2007. He has spread his Martial Art System World Wide for almost a decade. Wright who is still prime, personally trains his Team. Also, Austin is a dedicated Father, Educator and Role Model to thousands who has made a tremendous impact on the Martial Arts Industry. His popularity as a Martial Arts Leader has brought many athletes and competitors from all over New Jersey to compete on his team.

Wright states", it wasn't easy growing up as a skinny kid in the projects. He had to fight off bullies who would often underestimate him because of his size. Martial Arts helped him to control his Temper, work on conflict resolution, and focus on his future goals. This helped him to become a "Peaceful and Humble Warrior". Thus, Universal Warrior Arts was created.... with Peace before War in Mind...

"A Black Belt Is a White Belt Who Never Quit!"

Unknown Author

DISCLAIMER:
NO CLAIM IS MADE TO THE EXCLUSIVE RIGHT TO USE *"UNIVERSAL WARRIOR ARTS SYSTEM"* AND *"MEMBER OF THE U.W.A. FEDERATION OF AMERICA"* APART FROM MARK AS SHOWN ®

Web Address: www.uwa-martialarts.com

U.W.A. Martial Arts Black Belt Leadership Academy:

A.K.A. Universal Dojo of Self-Defense, Inc.

250 Broadway

Bayonne, New Jersey 07002

Phone Number: (201) 437-1820

1683 Kennedy Blvd.

Jersey City, NJ 07305

Phone Number: (201) 360-0951

For inquiries about registering your school or dojo under the U.W.A. Federation of America, contact the main headquarters.

universalwarriorarts@yahoo.com

<u>References</u>

The Bible

The Art of War by Sun Tzu

Universal Principles and Philosophy (World-Wide Cultures)

Personal Experience, Training, Competitions, and Seminars

Military Experience

The Kybalion (Hermetic Philosophy by "Three Initiates")

Forty-Three Years of Formal Training – World Wide

Street Survival Experiences

Various Arenas

Marion, J. B. (1999). *Anti-aging manual: The Encyclopedia of Natural Health.* South Woodstock, CT: Information Pioneers

Special Notes:

Illustrations By: Grandmaster Austin Wright, Sr.

Mr. Antonio Wilson

Mr. Tom Boassci

Editing By: Grandmaster Austin Wright, Sr., Dr. Dennis P. McCarthy, Josie Cleary, Marisol Cerdeira, Carmela Pallotta, and Anthony Bianciella Esq., Allen Woodman

Final Layout and Arrangement By: SIDEKICK Publications

Final Cover and Illustration Graphics By: SIDEKICK Publications / Allen Woodman

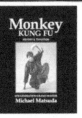

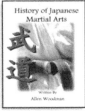

Made in the USA
Middletown, DE
09 May 2022